Surviving To Thriving When Life Gives You Lemons

Research: Sarah Chapman, James Morgan, Katerina Levy, Gregory Blackman and Olivia Cartwright.

Published in 2020

By Lovely Silks Publishing & Athena Publishing

Edited By Jacqueline Rose

All rights reserved. No part of this work may be reproduced or transmitted in any form or by any means, electronic or mechanical, including photocopying, recording, or by any information storage or retrieval system, without the prior written permission of the copyright owner and the publisher.

This book is presented solely for educational and entertainment purposes. The author and publisher are not offering it as legal, accounting, or other professional services advice. While best efforts have been used in preparing this book, the author and publisher make no representations or warranties of any kind and assume no liabilities of any kind with respect to the accuracy or completeness of the contents and specifically disclaim any implied warranties of merchantability or fitness of use for a particular purpose.

Neither the author nor the publisher shall be held liable or responsible to any person or entity with respect to any loss or incidental or consequential damages caused, or alleged to have been caused, directly or indirectly, by the information or programs contained herein. No warranty may be created or extended by sales representatives or written sales materials. Every company is different and the advice and strategies contained herein may not be suitable for your situation. You should always seek the services of a competent professional.

Also by Lovely Silks Publishing

Reboot Your Life

Reboot Your Life - Phoenix Edition

If I Can, You Can – Winners Edition

Successful Women in Business

Successful Women in Business – Coral Edition

Still Waters Run Deep

The Art Of Effective Communication

The Alternative Well-Being Sciences

Having It All At Fifty Plus

Having It All At Fifty Plus – Innovation Edition

How To Be Happy

Recipes That Make You Go Mmm…

Recycling and Renewable Energy

Weddings, Weddings, Weddings

Surviving To Thriving When Life Gives You Lemons

"My Biggest Motivation?

*Just to keep challenging myself.
I see life almost like one long university education that I never had
– every day I'm learning something new."* Richard Branson

All that we are is the result of what we have thought.
The mind is everything.
What we think, we become - Buddha

CONTRIBUTING AUTHORS

Clare Goodwin, Dr Stephanie Minchin, Jay Anderson,

Rebecca McQueen, Dessy Ohanians, Sarah Lloyd, Lenore Pearson,

Ketan Dattani, Orlaith Brogan, Carolyn King, Dr Deborah Lee,

CONTENTS

Introduction	17
Running A Business From Home, Offering An Insight On Steps We Can Take To Remain Healthy And Productive	20
Yoga as a Therapy: The Healing Power of Yoga to Support your Wellbeing During and After Corona Virus	34
In Captivity & Isolation, We Found Freedom	59
Stuck At Home? From Overwhelmed & Stressed To Engaged & Connected	68
How To Survive And Thrive The Corona Crisis - It's Time For Plan B!	83
The 5 Key Steps To Stay Happy And Healthy Whilst Running Your Business From Home	95

What Parents Need To Know About Children What Can Parents
& Children Do To Survive Self-Isolation, & Each Other & How To
Stay Creative & Keep Your Family Sane During Lockdown   104

Business In A Post-COVID-19 World And The Role Of AI In
Reinventing Business   115

A Frozen Life:
Re-Connecting To Motherhood During Lockdown   126

Balancing Children At Home, Maintaining Good Wellbeing For
All, Whilst Still Working And Home Schooling   138

Life Is An Adventure:
A Journey From The Darkness To The Light   152

Foods To Boost The Immune System   176

References   218

Introduction

Welcome to Surviving To Thriving When Life Gives You Lemons

This unique book has been written a chapter at a time by professionals from around the world sharing their collective inspirational knowledge and insights as we all work our way through this extraordinary experience of the Covid 19 pandemic.

Many of the basic ideas such as freedom of movement around our planet and human contact, which we all have taken for granted have now been removed from us at this time. While governments and scientists struggle to gain some sort of control over this deadly virus many of us are feeling stress, anxiety and overwhelm as we try to make sense of how we can carry on and move forward.

Our normal way of life no longer applies as we see our lives rapidly turned upside down. We as a human race have had to face challenges we'd never even considered or imagined. We've been forced to home school our children, work from home, been challenged to run a business from home with employees, while still effectively keeping our mental health and relationships intact.

With all challenges we have to be stronger when we are at our weakest or caught off balance. When you can't control what's happening we need to challenge ourselves to control the way we respond to what's happening. Challenges are what makes life interesting and overcoming them is what makes life meaningful. This is where we can become powerful and grow as we work our way through this unchartered water.

Surviving To Thriving When Life Gives You Lemons has been written by professional contributors from many different walks of life from around the world. Offering you some practical and valuable advice on how to maintain your health, business and well-being through these difficult times.

Surviving To Thriving When Life Gives You Lemons has been produced in an informative, conversational style with valuable, thought provoking advice from health and life coaches to real business people running real businesses from their homes.

Within the pages of this book you'll find it packed with valuable insights and advice that tackle some of the most common (and often not so common) problems associated with life at the present time in 2020.

Whether you're working from home, running your own business with or without employees or home schooling your children this book will help inspire and motive you back to your personal normal path in life.

Jacqueline Rose

Publisher, Lovely Silks Publishing

Running A Business From Home, Offering An Insight On Steps We Can Take To Remain Healthy And Productive

Running a business has its challenges at the best of times. Navigating through a crisis like a pandemic adds challenges that none of us could really be prepared for, especially for a business like Body & Spirit, which is based on face-to-face interactions between clients.

Once it became clear that social distancing would be important to help stop the spread of COVID-19, it was important that we adapted quickly so that we could continue to offer our core services. In addition, with myself and our team members all having young families at home to care for – and no formal childcare in place anymore – it was important to find an entirely new structure that would provide a balance between work and family life.

On top of everything else, I was very concerned that all of the hard work I had put into my own mental and emotional health was about to go out of the window through a shear lack of space and time. I was definitely feeling the fear on many levels!

Body & Spirit Before Coronavirus

At Body & Spirit our aim is to provide physical movement, mind-ful activity and spiritual practices that support people on their personal journey to health and happiness. One of the core values we hold is 'support' – for our clients, the wider community, and our team.

We want to support our clients on their own path of development and discovery. This has always been a very hands-on interaction; allowing strong connections to develop.

It is also important that we are there for each other behind the scenes. Through group interaction and easy communication, everyone from office workers to support workers, teachers and therapists, should have what they need to work happily and effectively, within their own work-life framework.

For our team I aim to allow, and facilitate where possible, each person to support themselves. Whether that be through continued personal development courses or supporting the balance of time at work with family needs.

The harmony of these three has always been fundamental to the running of Body & Spirit. Before even setting up the company, I wanted to be able to offer clients what they needed while managing my own needs for personal growth and time with my family. This was something I had previously found – and sometimes continue to find – very difficult. I was keen that going forwards, new team members coming on board would feel strongly about offering the best they could to our clients, while being able to have their own work-life balance needs met.

One of the other values dear to my heart is providing a polished service. I wanted the experience of coming to Body & Spirit to be easy; to be high quality and to feel genuine and personal. Until the coronavirus crisis began, this had always been achieved through a close 'hands on' approach. Both physically, using hands to guide the body itself, and emotionally, creating open channels of communication during, and in between face to face sessions.

Working Through A Pandemic

Now suddenly, the world had changed in a day and people were no longer able to have contact with each other. Continuing to run such a hands-on business was going to be a huge challenge. No longer could I have a physical connection with my clients, and yet potentially, the sudden and unexpected change in the world meant they may need their classes and therapies now more than ever. My beautiful childminder – who is like a second Mum to my four-year-old – our fabulous babysitter, and amazing nursery school teachers, who had all been instrumental in helping with our beautiful daughter (it takes a village, right?!), were no longer there to help. I was completely unable to connect face to face with the incredible team I was slowly building within and around Body & Spirit. And, I was also keenly aware that not only was my business in jeopardy, but if I was unable to pay others for their help, their businesses and incomes were at risk too.

I was faced with having to completely rethink the entire way I worked, make the seemingly huge changes necessary to keep Body & Spirit running, and figure out how, between my husband and I, how we could work fulltime jobs and be fulltime parents to our daughter.

My brilliant marketing manager and assistant, who I rely on to help me 'hold all the balls in the air', was in the same boat. She was trying to retain her business while her husband continued working outside of the home in a key worker role, and also looking after a two-year-old – with no additional daytime childcare. I needed her yet I wasn't sure I could afford her anymore, or that she could work in quite the same way.

Coping In A Crisis

The first three weeks of the virus threw up completely different experiences, with each week requiring very different energies, decisions and strategies. I was experiencing a rollercoaster of emotions for sure. Week one felt really tough. It was to be the 'doing and worrying' week. I was concerned for the health and wellbeing of our clients as they went through what was to be a very difficult time, and for the ability of Body & Spirit to cope financially.

For many different reasons, from concern about infection to their own financial uncertainties, some clients were making the decision to stop taking sessions for a while. Others wanted guidance and certainty in the ability of their sessions to provide what they needed, while keeping safe and healthy.

Within that first week, I made the decision to take the entire business online, keeping all classes running and even developing some new ones. I have to admit, I was sceptical that working from home in this way could be as effective. I wouldn't be able to just reach into the screen and be hands on. I know some clients had their reservations too, but I am happy to say, those who were unsure at first adapted quickly to our new way of working. I was particularly surprised at the effectiveness of sessions with private clients, where it was sometimes even easier to see via our online interactions what was going on within people's energy and bodies. I also had great feedback from clients who were equally surprised at how much they were enjoying their sessions and how grateful they were to be able to continue to keep themselves happy and healthy. I know that across the country and the world, many businesses were moving, online and I am sure this will be forever known as the time of 'Zoom'!

However, for me, this was not enough. I felt strongly that further plans and strategies were needed in order to maintain the supportive and polished service Body & Spirit offers.

Up until now a strong website had not been high on my list of priorities as there was always so much else to do. Now it has become an invaluable resource. My amazing husband (the creative and techy one of us) swiftly developed the existing small landing page into an amazing place where people could find lots of information. An extra 'resources' page was included with tips on using Zoom effectively, finding music and equipment that could be used at home during online classes, and offering short videos that could be used between sessions – to help with the inevitable aches and pains created by working from home and living in a stressful time.

As information from the government was ever changing, I also began publishing videos, emails and social media posts with regular updates. I wanted to be present and to bring clarity in uncertain times. This kind of work was something I had always avoided, partly for fear of bombarding people with information and partly for fear of not doing it well enough – or not looking as good as others! Suddenly none of this seemed to matter. Everyone trying to maintain a business was in the same position. We needed to be able to support our clients and customers, and few were able to have luxurious or beautiful backdrops, makeup artists and hairstylists to create a stunning video. Freed from these irrational fears, I was surprised at how producing extra content, or as I like to see it, 'using my voice', wasn't as bad as I expected. I still don't love this kind of work; it's why I am a teacher and guide, and not in marketing, but running a business requires both, and a fear has been lifted – a little.

I was also very keen to personally call or connect with as many individual clients as possible, particularly those that I would not now see for a while. For some it was important that this happened within the immediate 24 to 48 hours of that first week, for others it would be something I would do over the course of the coming weeks. I wanted to simply chat, check on how they were doing and to discuss any questions or concerns they may have had. This was time consuming but was very well received.

Finally, I dearly wished to be able to help those who were not our clients and needed support too. The idea to offer free online meditations to anyone was almost instant. These were broadcast live on social media most days of the week, at a time that helped people develop a good daily routine and recorded for those needing them at a different time.

Again, the feedback was great. I was in tears reading some of the short messages I received from people who I had never met before telling me how the meditations were helping support them through a very challenging time.

****

After the initial explosion of activity (and sleep deprivation), weeks two and three bought about very different challenges.

As things became a little less hectic, I had some time to think. In many ways this was harder. The fears began to surface. I wasn't yet finished with building the Body & Spirit dream and yet it may all come tumbling down. How would our family cope? What would be the effect on my own mental health? And of course, could I bring in enough money, and would the business survive financially?

I experienced the emotional tug-of-war between shrinking, ceasing to pay for everything and everyone bar the absolute basic essentials, and – thinking abundantly – knowing that if I could continue to run the business as fully as possible and to continue to pay for as much as was sensible, I could sustain Body & Spirit and maybe even flourish.

In the end, slowly and inevitably some of the basic decisions were taken by the government and, as things shut down nationally for our initial lockdown period, I was no longer able to use studios, or to take unnecessary journeys – let alone make face to face contact with anyone outside my household. This clarity made many of the decisions simple. However, I still felt inner turmoil about how to continue working with other practitioners and businesses. I did need them, but could I afford them?

Throughout my adult life, I have struggled to step away from feeling small and restricted, or to see my worth. I had, and still do have, a fiercely strong work ethic – of which I am proud and give thanks to my amazing parents for. However, I could never quite seem to find a work-life balance, my purpose, or real happiness. I wasn't even sure what those things looked like. Life felt like a lot of hard work for small reward and something had always prevented me from really growing and discovering. In recent years however, my body began to give me great big signs that things were really not working. It was then that I embarked on a personal journey of discovery and growth. Along the way, life introduced me to the 'right' people with whom I developed some important and supportive relationships for which I will always be grateful. One of these was the work undertaken with an energy healer, and another with a like-minded business coach – both of whom are so much more than their titles suggest. Along with close friends and colleagues, they have helped immeasurably with my personal and business journeys. These connections have allowed me to understand myself better, to truly see who I am, what I am good at and what I want to offer. These were the people who had really helped me and my business to flourish.

And yet, at a time of real crisis these were some of the people I was considering pushing away because I wanted to hold onto the money I had. Through conversations with them, others and myself, I was reminded that health and growth can only come when you continue to invest (however that looks) in yourself. I was reminded to always ask the questions: are you making this decision out of fear or abundance? What do you want to achieve in this time? And, how do you want to be remembered after this time? Realisation also dawned that the connections I had with these people were the same connections I had with my clients. Whilst Body & Spirit may not be a front-line service, people would need what I offered, now and especially in the future. I wanted to be able to continue to work with and support my clients, and I knew that my healer and coach wanted to continue to support me.

Daily I changed my mind as to whether I could bring myself to take a leap, spend if I sensibly could, and think abundantly. At the time the decision seemed hard. Looking back, I am grateful I chose what seemed like the more difficult path. Spending and growing when many were hunkering down. The choices I made here completely changed the course of my life through the coronavirus outbreak and, without others I may well have trodden a different path.

*****

In terms of balancing home life with the demands of work, it took a little longer than a week, or even two, to develop a private routine that allowed our household to function, to remain sane and stay healthy. Important conversations were necessary; from the 'money talk' to 'this is what I need talk'.

On a practical level it became increasingly clear that we needed a 'how to live and work at home, and not kill each other' strategy. I needed to use different rooms for different jobs. The living room was the only room big enough to teach a class in, but this meant kicking the family out. For the meditations I needed a space where I would not have a four-year-old coming in to ask for help on the toilet! The kitchen became my husband's office – not ideal, and the dining chairs were not helping his neck – or mood!

There was so much to do that the easy road was; working, begrudgingly finding time to play, shouting at each other, letting the stress build up and never leaving the house. We had to talk; about family time, getting out of the house and money worries – and we needed to order Daddy a proper office chair!

We developed a schedule of who was working where and when. During working days, even though we were under one roof, my husband and I became a bit like ships passing in the night, one working while one was doing family time and then swapping. Of course, we had to work within the obvious constraints; I had to be teaching at the times classes were needed, and my husband had to be at his desk and online during traditional office hours. We sat with a pen and paper and worked out a schedule. This worked well, but no matter how well we planned, there were always going to be those times when we both needed to be in meetings and classes at the same time. Our daughter became famous on her Daddy's Zoom meetings and I am not ashamed to say that 'Nanny iPad' certainly played a role!

As a balance to this weekly schedule, it was obvious that taking complete time out for the family, and for ourselves, was going to be really important for both physical and mental health. In one small respect we were lucky that all of this was happening during a beautiful blooming springtime. Having the garden as an extra 'room' on the house was heaven sent. So, organising personal time on paper was fairly straightforward; scheduled walks, proper days off and planned individual activities (now all online of course). The greatest challenge I found with this was the mental switch between work, family and me time. I have always found this difficult anyway, but usually there is travel between work and home, and time to gently transition your headspace. Now time between things and away from each other was gone. For me there was – and still is – no easy fix for this. I still find myself thinking about one thing when I am doing another or struggling with the switch of pace between different activities. This is stressful, especially when deadlines loom. I particularly worry about the, "I'll be with you in just a minute," that my daughter hears far too often, and I have had to accept that sometimes, things just take longer than I would like. It's easy to think that everyone else has it sorted, but this is my story to live, I can only do what I can, and I know I am not superhuman. So, I try to give myself a break.

****

Speaking of which... For our relationship, my husband and I had to have two important conversations. How could we give each other a break, and how we would manage our finances? Otherwise, we may well have been taking a permanent break! I have heard it joked that with everyone living in such close quarters together, it is the divorce lawyers who will be coming out of this time most well off!

Firstly, we needed to give each other the time to do the things that sustain us as happy humans. For me that was taking time with my spiritual and physical practices, for him, tinkering with his car and bashing his drum kit (I am sure the neighbours are glad for muting pads!). For both of us together it was time spent working and playing in the garden.

Secondly, we needed to have 'the money talk'. How much did we have? How much were we likely to earn in this time? What were our priorities and what could we live without? How could we pool our resources differently from normal if needed? We also found that this was not a one-time conversation. As the situation changed over the weeks, both nationally and personally, we were to repeat this discussion on a couple of occasions.

****

Finally, having worked out the finances, and having faced the spending fears, I knew I needed to continue to work with my assistant if I could. Thankfully, due to the values that Body & Spirit holds, we already had a good foundation. We knew what each other needed, what personal boundaries were in place and what the work-life balance looked like for each other (usually meaning that something would always take longer than expected on my part!). All we really needed to do was look at any specifics that needed change. I set in motion weekly catch up meetings. Not too long, just enough time to check in on how she was doing in herself, where we were at with current jobs, new ideas and innovations, what needed to be done going forwards, and if we both had the tools and support required to do the job at hand. We also changed our 'available to work' hours in light of our new home situations. The structure and boundaries put in place gave us confidence in what we were doing and personally, allowed me to turn my head off when not in those 'working hours'.

Moving Forwards

There are going to be many more challenges in front of us I am sure – already things are changing in the world again. The transition from life now, to the new life awaiting us all is going to be long and will, I am sure, require continued innovation and renewed perspectives. It may be even harder as we all go through many gradual and subtle changes and the government guidelines are inevitably less utilitarian and absolute.

For Body & Spirit, it has been incredibly difficult at times, but the changes have taught me a lot; about myself, about the things I can and want to achieve and about the things I want the company to offer. I am sure that many of the changes made in recent weeks will remain and I can see the potential for some new and exciting developments on the horizon that I never would have expected. Knowing that we have adapted and innovated so well, gives me confidence that we can see our way through to the road ahead.

In many ways the fear now is of going back. So much sadness and difficulty has been experienced and endured by so many, and none of us would have wished this on anyone. I only hope that going forwards we can, all of us, continue to support each other, take care of the world around us, and make decisions with love, not fear, greed or selfishness.

Gratitude

I hope that some of the ideas and stories here are helpful. I have certainly not been able to devise and do all of this on my own. Never have I been more aware of the amazing people I have around me or more grateful for their own individual gifts.

To those of you joining classes, sessions and meditations: I would like to say a big thank you for all of the fantastic feedback and continued support. It has been a pleasure to work with you. To the amazing people in and around Body & Spirit, your ideas, feedback and support has been invaluable. You may not have always had the same point of view, but you have all held up the mirror and given me the sounding board I needed to flourish and grow in a time that could have been so different. Finally, to my family and friends, I could not do what I do without your love, support and very often practical and unpaid assistance. I love and cherish you all.

Clare Goodwin

About The Author

Clare Goodwin is founder of **Body & Spirit**, which provides classes, workshops and retreats to support people on their journey to health, happiness, and a better quality of life. Clare's work is firmly rooted in the understanding that everything is connected; body, mind, and spirit.

Clare began her working life as a professional dancer, before becoming a personal trainer. However, the fitness arena felt restrictive, and she became more aware of the need to work with people on strengthening and improving their bodies in a more holistic way. Through discovering the practice of Pilates, Clare's world opened up. She was able to help people get stronger and fitter, improve postural balance and functional ability, and get rid of aches and pains that had plagued them for years.

Over the coming years Clare was diagnosed with Type 1 diabetes, married the love of her life, made the big move from London to the country, and had her beautiful daughter. She loved her life but despite preaching it, wasn't always happy or healthy.

At this point she embarked on a slow and gradual journey of learning and personal development. From discovering the power of meditation to understanding her moon and menstrual cycle, to discovering personality patterning, finding the chakra, hara line and core, this whole new world strongly informed the way Clare wanted to work.

By including this deeper mental and emotional approach, her Pilates classes have expanded and developed. She has found a passion for the incredible results of Yamuna Body Rolling, and meditation now plays an important role as a stand-alone offering, and as part of physical classes and workshops. Her calling is in helping people on their own personal journey to health and happiness with a particular gift of focusing on the body, how it can communicate with you and tell you what it needs.

To find out more about Clare & Body & Spirit visit:

http://www.clare-goodwin.com/

Yoga as a Therapy: The Healing Power of Yoga to Support your Wellbeing During and After Corona Virus

With the boom of yoga in the wellbeing industry, the essence of its practice is easily masked by disproportionate popularity of slim-line smoothies, luscious leggings and the promotion of a 'yoga body'. Despite this commercialisation marking yoga on everybody's map, the masses that practice mainly view yoga as a physical activity. The shapes, the 'peak pose', the 'asanas'. However, underlying the carefully crafted sequences and yoga studios sprawling urban landscapes and rural retreats, are the values that offer yoga as a way of living, an art form.

This chapter explores yoga as a therapeutic tool for self-healing, as part of collective healing. The philosophical roots of yoga are detailed and scientific research is discussed to evidence the positive effects of yoga on physical, mental, emotional and spiritual health. Rebuilding connection and hope through yoga following the traumatic global impact of the coronavirus leads to consideration of how to practice yoga, who yoga is for and moving forward to 'come back home' through yoga.

1. **Yoga: A Therapeutic Tool to Heal**

'The goal of yoga was originally to provide a guide for wholeness, happiness, and well-being.' Feuerstein (2003).
The root of the word yoga means 'to yoke' or 'to harness', and in this context means the integration of mind, body and spirit, with a traditional

practice leading towards the transcendence of the self (Feuerstein, 2003, p4.). Yoga practices are believed to facilitate self-transformation by developing physical strength, balance of the autonomic nervous systems and a calm, tranquil mind (Kaley-Isley, et al., 2010). Birdee, et al. (2008) report a growing trend of yoga as a complementary medicine in the USA, particularly for children; with yoga ranked as fifth out of 39 complementary medicine practices in its perceived effectiveness (Tsao, et al., 2005). Mind-body medicine is highlighted as directly impacting health by an interaction between brain, mind, body and behaviour, working on mental, emotional, social, spiritual and behavioural factors (Kaley-Isley, et al., 2010).

What Is Yoga Therapy?

Yoga Therapy was first defined in the 1920s by Kuvalyananda who advocated that medical conditions may be treated at both the physical and physiological level with the therapeutic effects of yoga.

The British Council of Yoga Therapists (BCYT) (http://www.bcyt.co.uk/) highlights that *'Yoga Therapy is Yoga where there is a specific need or needs. Yoga Therapy views the person as a whole; an integrated system of mind, body, emotional and spiritual aspects. Yoga Therapy can address different aspects as appropriate, to promote healing and improve health.'* The BCYT describes how Yoga Therapy can *'encourage a quietening of the mind to help deal with stress or anxiety or to find space inside where we can begin to feel more comfortable and peaceful'*.

Unlike talking therapies, Yoga Therapy does not need to know the story and explore the background, it simply works with the person as they are and the symptoms as they present. This enables the therapeutic work to connect with the individual as their whole self, and not be defined by their past experiences or diagnostic label. The International Association of Yoga Therapists (IAYT) suggests that through the applications of the teachings and practices of yoga, the process of Yoga Therapy may *'empower individuals to progress toward health and well-being'*.

The Kosha Model

According to yogic tradition, every individual has 5 'bodies', made up of increasingly finer grade energies from the external layer to the inner body. In an ancient yogic text, the Taittiriya Upanishads defines these bodies as 'koshas', meaning 'layers' or 'sheaths'. It is contended that the energy of each sheath is related to the next layer, working from the outside layer to the core, such that an imbalance in one sheath has an inevitable impact on the next. In order to maintain a state of inner equilibrium and peace across physical, mental, emotional and spiritual functioning, each kosha must be in balance.

The Kosha Model Is Described As Follows:

1. *Annamaya kosha* - 'Anna' (food) - the outermost physical layer; the physical body as an outer shell; concerned with the food that we eat as resourcing energy to fuel our system. This directly links to nutrition and lifestyle guidance, such as exercise and dietary habits e.g. alcohol, smoking, substances.
2. *Pranamaya kosha* - 'Prana' (energy) - the subtle energy layer; the automatic processes and systems within our body that are essential to life, including respiration, circadian rhythms, digestion, restorative and regenerative processes for cell growth, immune

3. functioning. This may consider how to regulate sleep, heart rate and blood pressure and all autonomic responses to stress as part of the fight or flight response.
4. *Manomaya kosha* - 'Mano' (mind) - the psychological layer; the inner workings of mental and emotional processes in regards to thinking styles, thought content, how we feel and the ability to be present rather than negatively caught in the past or future. Yoga can identify thought patterns, mindfulness of thought, shape and change behaviours, and promote a state of being soothed rather than critical.
5. *Vijnanamaya kosha* - 'Vij' (wisdom) - the higher mind; this translates as discernment, and the power of judgement, and what distinguishes humans from animals. This relates to morals, values and ethics, one's personality, and the ways in which one chooses to live their life.
6. *Anandamaya kosha* - 'Ananda' (bliss) - the subtle most body; higher states of consciousness, linked to ideas of something greater than ourselves. In yoga, a sense of spirituality is not necessary and we can use the idea of this kosha to consider what brings the most joy into one's life.

The benefits of the kosha model applied through yoga are that it encompasses all aspects of being, in a holistic view, whilst acknowledging the inter-related dynamic of each layer on the next of our experience. The kosha model is inclusive, such that any individual of every aspect of diversity is able to use the model to apply to their own unique experience.

Tate (2003) highlights how the kosha model of yoga therapy focuses on all levels of the person and, if integrated into healthcare, yoga therapy may provide a foundation of healing by which individuals can be empowered to seek positive wellbeing across the physical, psychological, energetic and spiritual aspects of themselves.

Therefore, it is contended that *'Yoga therapy would be very useful as an adjuvant therapy for many conditions to which modern medicine has only a partial answer'* (Varma & Raju, 2012, p.2).

2. **The Philosophy Of Yoga: Understanding Yoga's True Roots In The Modern World**

'The nature of yoga is to shine light into the darkest areas of the body.' Jason Crandell.

The theory and practice of yoga are detailed in The Yoga Sutras, compiled by the sage Patanjali between 500 and 400 BC, outlining 196 different sutras, as a lesson of truth, shared from ancestors and previous generations as guiding principles. In seminal yogic texts, philosophers outline the 'eight limbs of yoga' as acts of self-study, encouraging ways of living a moral life in relation to self and others. These principles are the *'Yamas'* (social restraints) and *'Niyamas'* (self-disciplines), encouraged to be observed every moment in daily life, with the aim to purify the body and the mind in order to establish inner peace and calm.

The practice of yoga is an offering of a way of being, beyond the mat. The guiding principles we can apply to our ways of living. So how can observing the Yamas and Niyamas support your wellbeing during and after Corona Virus?

The Yamas

Ahimsa - non-harming, non-violence. This is a practice of not causing pain or suffering to oneself, anyone else, or any living being. In this period of time, are you doing things that don't serve you? Sometimes it's not about explicit acts of 'self-harm' yet smaller unconscious acts or thoughts that contribute to suffering. Over-eating to cure boredom or drinking excess of alcohol to escape reality? Speaking to yourself in unkind ways as that inner critic gets louder telling you, you are 'not enough'? Or perhaps releasing frustration and stress onto someone else? The ethic of Ahimsa calls to question doing good by yourself and others to not inflict any suffering or distress, and treat yourself and others in the highest good.

Satya ~ truthfulness. This is a practice of honesty, to overcome deceit, denial and lies. Sometimes the hardest part is the honesty we need to show ourselves, particularly in the areas that we have blocked or overlooked, where we don't want to know or accept the truth. Satya is about voicing and accepting reality as it is now, and being aligned with your own values.

Asteya ~ non-stealing. Not taking something that is not yours. Practicing acceptance for what you have and not longing for what you don't. With the idea that worry and anxiety are the thieves of joy, worrying about the future (especially life after Corona-Virus) is stealing you away from the experience of the present moment and the gifts it has to offer. Given that there is much about this wider pandemic that is beyond our internal control, don't allow worry to steal your inner peace.

Aparigraha ~ non-attachment. A pure process of letting go. Thinking about this pandemic and the multiple losses that many of us may have experienced, it is a tough task to not attach to our old ways of life, be it job, financial security, routines, social gatherings. Perhaps we will serve ourselves best to not attach to the pre-Covid 19 life and become better adjusted to a 'new normal'.

Brahmacharya - maintenance of vitality. In earlier Hinduism and Buddhism, Brahmacharya was more associated with sexual abstinence and celibacy. Although some of us may be in a socially enforced celibacy due to constraints on socialisation with dating temporarily not an option, we could reframe the practice of Brahmacharya to not giving our energy to where it is undeserved. Consider where your energy is directed, how it is spent, what it is drained by, and how preserving aspects of your energy you are better guided to live more fully.

The Niyamas

Saucha ~ cleanliness. This is about purity of body, mine, spirit and environment, and creating a 'clean' inside world. Throughout life we may have picked up bad habits, eat or drink toxic substances, create mess at home, and receive stress from the world around us. Through a process of cleansing we are detoxifying the negativities we have collected over time. Perhaps this means de-cluttering the space at home, not-hoarding objects, eating healthy and organic food, or directing attention towards positive thoughts.

Santosha ~ contentment. The misguidance of 'happiness' in the modern world is that it is easily misplaced to external things, in an attachment to attributes. The job title, the money, the house, the building blocks of the physical. Contentment means inner peace. A soul searching, which is much harder to find, and of course, a state that is transient, ever-changing with the ebbs and flow of life, not necessarily a permanent way of being. Consider what is important to you, in your world and your wellbeing; ask yourself why; and let your actions guide you there. Because peace and happiness is an ever-changing state whose home constantly lies within.

Tapas ~ purification through discipline. The word 'tapas' is derived from meanings of 'to burn', with a fiery quality linked to passion. In order to cultivate more discipline in our lives, and tend to what keeps our inner fires burning, we need to burn off old impurities and destructive habits in order to make space for more growth. Using this period of time may be a point of reassessment; how do you want to live your life, what areas require more attention, effort and control and what changes can you make to allow for something positively different?

Svadhyaya ~ self-study. 'To recollect the self'. Studying the self is an art of going in. Becoming more aware of your behavioural patterns, thought processes, emotional states and with a process of self-reflexivity inviting curious questioning to ask 'why?' Building awareness to better know ourselves can lead to increased understanding of why we live how we live, and consequently be the catalyst for change if that is what we desire.

Ishvara Pranidhana ~ 'to surrender'. An act of devotion to a higher power. Disclaimer: in my view, this does not have to be about religion, faith or specific identity; yet an act of giving to a higher purpose. For some, yes, perhaps this means God, a god, or the universe. To others, an act of surrender to a higher purpose may mean devoting time, effort or energy to the wider community, a charitable cause, or any other act of giving.

The Yamas and Niyamas offer a big possibility for transformation. At first, they may seem like words which are translatable, too foreign or unfamiliar, literally speaking a different language. However, this is about *how* we relate to the Yamas and Niyamas and what we do with them in daily life, how they transfer with meaning, principle and practice to support our own positive wellbeing. For even small steps, practiced little by little, are the building blocks for change.

3. **The Science Of Yoga:**
   Research On The Therapeutic Effects Of Yoga On Wellbeing

'Yoga is not a religion. It is a science, science of wellbeing… science of integrating body, mind and soul' (Amit Ray).

The Brief Science Of Yoga Therapy

There is a growing research evidence-base which highlights some of the adaptive physiological, neurological and psychological changes hypothesised as a positive impact of yoga. Yoga therapy seeks to find balance within the autonomic nervous system, by downregulating the hypothalamic pituitary adrenal (HPA) axis, reducing the release of cortisol (stress hormone), decreasing sympathetic nervous system (SNS - stress) activity and increasing the parasympathetic nervous system (PNS - relax) whilst building the 'window of tolerance' to distress. Research suggests that the greater the flexibility between the sympathetic and parasympathetic nervous system, and the greater heart rate variability, the greater the resilience of emotional wellbeing and mental health.

The vagus nerve plays an important role in the relaxation response. It is the tenth cranial nerve which 'wanders' across the body's vital organs, including the heart, lungs and digestive tract, and has more afferent nerves than efferent nerves; this means the vagus nerve carries more information from the body to the brain than vice versa. Through the practice of yoga, breathing practices and body movement, the vagus nerve can influence the PNS, such as slowing the heart rate, slowing the breath and prompting the relaxation response.

In the Polyvagal Theory, Stephen Porges (2009) proposes that myelinated nerves within the vagus significantly influence prosocial behaviour, social engagement and bonding; it is suggested that this occurs when new neural pathways are created during feelings of safety and connection. Mason and Gerbarg (2018) suggest that safety can be created in yoga therapy by stimulating interoceptive experiences of movement and breathing.

On a neurological level, yoga may encourage the amygdala (brain's 'alarm bell') to quieten down and communication between brain neural pathways may be improved and more efficient. This is particularly relevant given that brain structures such as the prefrontal cortex have been found to reduce in size, volume and functioning in individuals with mental health difficulties, with an overactive hyper-vigilant amygdala.

For individuals with mental health difficulties, and specifically trauma, Van der Kolk (2014) suggests that yoga is a tool to re-educate the mind to feel and tolerate physical sensations, such that with increased emotional and physical awareness, one may reconnect with themselves.

Yoga As Therapy, Makes Good Medicine

Robold (2002, p.81) states *'yoga as therapy… makes good medicine, and is a valuable compliment or alternative to traditional treatment'*. Given that we are living in a time of mass uncertainty, multiple unknowns in various strands of our 'normal' lives with a potential for us all to be impacted psychologically from the challenge this pandemic brings, yoga can be a tool of self-medication.

The current research evidence-base shares a wealth of insightful and promising results on the positive effects of yoga. As the one of the multiple underlying symptomologies of mental distress is emotional dysregulation, there is a growing body of research that *'supports the belief that yoga benefits physical and mental health via downregulation of the hypothalamic-pituitary-adrenal (HPA) axis and the sympathetic nervous system'* (Ross and Thomas, 2010, p.3). This means that yoga works directly on the nervous system to lower states of stress. As a state of stress is a normal reaction to the direct and indirect consequences of coronavirus, increased stress is something that we are likely all experiencing. It is hypothesised that through attention and control of the body and breath, yoga seeks to down-regulate the stress response and work on physiological, cognitive and emotional systems, as well as build our own individual capacity to self-soothe.

Yoga invites a sense of mental and emotional awareness and self-regulation skills via breathing techniques and body postures; it is hypothesised that such practices elicit adaptive neural and mental responses that result in improved behaviour and emotional regulation

(Greenberg and Harris, 2012). Thus, it is suggested that yoga is not only a recreational activity yet also a rehabilitative tool to develop a healthy body and mind (Greenberg and Harris, 2012).

Brown and Gerbarg (2005) advocate for the benefits of mind-body practices for mental and physical health difficulties. It is suggested that a neurophysiological model of yogic breathing can alleviate anxiety, depression, stress, post-traumatic stress and stress-related medical illnesses through mechanisms which increase parasympathetic drive and calm stress response systems (Brown and Gerbarg, 2005).

Khalsa, et al. (2012), leading expert in mind-body medicine and Assistant Professor at Harvard Medical School specialising in yoga therapy, explains that yoga works on both the cognitive (mind) and physiological (body) stress. It is suggested that with conscious control of the body and breath through yoga postures, changes in the brain encourage present-moment thinking and quieten down the brain's 'alarm bell', to reduce negative chatter and less reactivity to the cycle of stress.

White (2012) suggests that yoga may be viewed as a behavioural intervention learnt to ride the turbulence of life in order to build resilience and protect people from the deleterious effects of stress. Self-regulation abilities are highlighted as a key component of yoga, enabling individuals to calm their bodies and emotions, build mastery and increase their repertoire of healthy living skills (Kaley-Isley, et al., 2010).

By cultivating an internal locus of control, Hagen and Nayar (2014) suggest that attention is shifted inwards to self-awareness, allowing individuals to learn how to monitor and manage their own cues and emotions, encouraging healthy and balanced living. Tate (2003) advocates that yoga can help us to overcome a variety of emotional and psychological difficulties through conscious and deliberate examination of the self through each level of the five koshas. Furthermore, Wei (2015) states that yoga therapy may be beneficial across the age spectrum and help to foster important skills in self-control, discipline, flexibility and creativity. Büssing, et al. (2012) highlight the beneficial supportive/adjunct treatment of yoga as part of a self-care behavioural treatment, associated with life-long skills, enhancing self-efficacy and self-confidence.

Yoga as a complementary medicine is a mind and body practice with focus on wholeness and healing. Weaver and Darragh (2015) commend yoga as embodying all modalities required to promote mental health and self-regulation skills. Therefore, it can be viewed that yoga as a form of self-therapy may be a positive complementary activity, as a non-pharmacological approach with few risks, inclusive and accessible for all, relatively inexpensive, non-stigmatising of human experience, supportive of human connection, speaks a universal language, can be fun and playful and empowering of individuals to manage their own healthcare. Therefore, yoga can empower us to overcome the adverse effects of the trauma of Corona Virus at a cognitive, physical, psychological, affective, interpersonal and behavioural level.

4. The Context Of Corona-Virus: The Impact Of Loss And Trauma, And Re-Establishing Hope And Connection Through Yoga

'Never doubt that a small group of thoughtful, committed citizens can change the world; indeed, it's the only thing that ever has'. Margaret Mead.

Nothing could quite have fully prepared us for the magnitude of the pandemic. Invisible and powerful. With effects from the individual to international level. We are being pushed into a space of sitting with uncertainty, unknowns in every direction and aspects of life, and an aftermath with consequences on personal, community and global health and economy. The context of coronavirus has caused disruption to 'normal life' akin to 'community trauma' i.e. a shared experience of a traumatic event across a community (Hobfell, et al., 2007).

We are experiencing direct and indirect consequences of loss, individually and within society, and the routine and socialisation of our daily lives have been forced to change with immediate effect. Some of us will be mourning the death of loved ones, with unexpected bereavements. At the centre of the context of corona-virus is loss. Loss of the life as we knew it. We will all be managing similar psychological processes to this loss, and between us will find our own variety of ways to cope and live through this trauma.

This is about transition. The 'process or period of change.' As human beings, we seek stability as it brings safety and comfort. However, we also evolve and grow from change. Throughout the life course we transition through multiple periods of change as we constantly navigate relationships, home life, education, employment, locations, health... the list is endless. The Law of Impermanence highlights that nothing is permanent and change and constant movement are the only guarantee. By moving beyond our comfort zone, widening our 'window of tolerance', and adapting to different 'stresses' we overcome challenges to establish something new. This is exactly our calling in this period of change. If we are suddenly forced to let go of the yesterday, how can we accept the now as we know it and welcome a brighter tomorrow?

The answer lies in collective action and community connection. For a collective trauma requires a collective response. Research shows that despite taking time to recover to a sense of safety, community trauma navigates the private and public space by bringing people together. Furthermore, Pynoos, et al. (1999) state that many who survive a trauma adaptively integrate their experience and develop normally. Hobfell, et al. (2007) suggest that the promotion of recovery from a community trauma involves establishing a sense of safety (with routines, regular information), promoting calm (relaxation techniques), promoting self and collective efficacy (to increase a sense of control and coping), promoting connection (positive and supportive relationships) and promoting hope (to build a better future).

Foucault views self-care as a 'political act'. Self-care is important, yet it is only sustainable if it is connected across people over time; with collective responsibility. When we start to be more accountable for ourselves and our own actions, we are better able to attend to the wider responsibility of those around us, be it family, friends, local neighbourhood or community, we become more socially responsible and connected. This is a call to move beyond self-care to collective care at the community level.

As a collective, we can create a communal story that reinforces our resilience. A story, that not only talks about suffering, yet a story that voices our survival. Pain, difficulties and challenges that we may continue to experience following this period of time is an exact demonstration of what we value and what we continue to live for. When we view ourselves and community as survivors, we start to notice exactly where our strengths lie. And it is these strengths that carry us forward. The Law of Relationships states that we are all connected; we share the same experiences, feel the same emotions, and through such challenges regardless of how or where we live, we are here to help one another learn and grow.

Yoga can offer that sense of connection. The practice of yoga invites a sense of belonging, as part of a wider community, be it next to someone on the yoga mat having journeyed through the same class together or a wider set of philosophical values with unity at the heart. The word 'Yoga' in Sanskrit translates as 'unite'; a practice which not only unites the practitioner with their own body, breath, mind and spirit, yet offers a unity with others. Yoga allows people to be drawn together in a relationship of their shared experience of yoga. This is a connection that we crave as social beings. Whether it is about the yoga practice itself or not, yoga offers itself a place where people can feel present, heard, voiced, accepted and truly come back 'home' into themselves. This is where the healing happens. And when we are feeling more grounded, stable and resilient on the inside, we are better able to ride out the chaos and turmoil going on the outside, and be part of a wider collective around us. Therefore, yoga lends itself to a process of self-healing and collective healing.

5. Your Yoga Practice: Starting The Journey

'If you practice yoga every day with perseverance, you will be able to face the turmoil of life with steadiness and maturity.' B.K.S Iyengar (2007).

Yoga Practice (Physical postures / 'asanas')

With the notion that the body benefits from movement, many view yoga as a physical practice. It is beyond the scope of the chapter to name every style of yoga and the benefits of each pose. Particularly given that beyond the commonalities of the physical benefits, are the gifts of unique experiences. Yes practicing yoga may make you more physically flexible and strong and aid recovery from an injury, but the physical poses are also working much more subtly on an emotional and energetic level. Through deeper physiological, neurological and psychological processing, yoga enables us to establish a different relationship with our body and how it moves. Moving, from the thinking mind into the feeling body.

From the standing pose that grounds us to the present moment to the Warrior pose that empowers, from the deep hip opener which prompts an emotional release to the heart opening pose that softens, every part of physical movement resonates more deeply on the inner psyche and emotional experience with more practice over time. As Judith Lasseter (2016) describes, the practice of yoga is a means of creating space in our bodies and minds for contentment to live within us.

Breathing Techniques ('Pranayama')

When we breathe more fully and deeply, we begin to breathe at a slower rate and make greater use of our lung capacity increasing the oxygen circulating our body and nourishing our cells. The breath is a messenger between the brain and body. Breathing slowly becomes a vehicle for reducing the stress response; when breathing slowly for 3 minutes or more, the body is transported into states of relaxation (moving from sympathetic/stress activity to parasympathetic/relaxation response).

The Below Breathing Techniques Are An Ideal Beginners Guide:

- **Belly breathing** - to draw fuller breathes down into 'the belly'; INHALE the ribs lift up and out, diaphragm pulls down, lungs expand; EXHALE the reverse

- **Longer exhale** - e.g. INHALE for the count of 4, EXHALE for count of 6-8
- **Equal breathing** (square) with pause (retention) - e.g. INHALE 4, pause 4, EXHALE 4, pause 4
- **Coherent breathing** - lowering the breathing rate to 5 breaths per minute
- **Ujjahi breathing** - the 'victorious breath', creating an ocean like sound; calms the mind and builds heat in the body

Mindfulness And Meditation

The Buddha was asked 'What have you gained from meditation? He replied 'Nothing! However, let me tell you what I have lost: anger, anxiety, depression and insecurity'.

There are multiple myths about 'emptying the mind', not 'being spiritual' or not being able to 'sit still' that create barriers to the very simplicity and challenge of sitting alone with one's mind. Mindfulness is a practice of noticing, being present with and not reacting to the constant changes within and around us. Mindfulness teaches us how to tolerate the pleasant and unpleasant equally, with an acceptance of the impermanent nature of both. With the notion that the quieter you become the more you hear, in a practice of meditation we can learn to be still and let life happen. Rather than get caught in a conflict, struggle and cycle of stress, we can move with the ebbs and flow of life as they unfold.

'*Yogas chitta vritti nirodhah*' translates as '*Yoga is the removal of the fluctuations of the mind*'. Allowing the fluctuations of our mind to rise and fall invites us to pause, to look at our shadows, and build a different relationship with our internal landscape. When we are more able to examine what is going on the inside, we heighten awareness and learn acceptance, enabling us to be responsive rather than reactive in our thoughts, feelings and behaviours.

Be Curious About Your Yoga Practice…. Enhance Your Awareness Through Reflective Thinking Or Journaling….

- How do you prefer to practice yoga, alone or with others, online or in class, led by a teacher or self-practice?
- What aspects of yoga bring you most pleasure?
- What do you notice about your breath when you practice yoga?
- How does your body feel with yoga as you move and make shapes?
- What differences do you notice in your experience of movement and stillness?
- Have you experienced any unique moments of change during yoga?
- What lessons have you been learning about yourself from yoga?
- In what way is yoga helpful or healing in your life?
- What values do you connect with from yoga that supports your daily life?
- Moving forward, how can your practice of yoga enhance positive mental, physical and emotional wellbeing for you?

6. Diversity In Yoga: Yoga For Everybody And Every Body

'Yoga is an essential tool in personal transformation, from the inside out, but also includes critical social justice'. Yoga Body Coalition.

Yoga is for anyone and everyone. It is an inclusive practice that looks beyond diversity and seeks to connect with the individual as they are, regardless of age, gender, shape, size, ability, ethnicity, race and culture, and more. In the simplest form, if you have a body and a breath, then you can access yoga on some level.

There is a need for inclusivity and equal opportunities to develop positive social and emotional skills for everybody across all socio-demographic contexts, at individual and group level. Individuals and families living in disadvantaged communities face significant, persistent and increasing health inequalities compared to their counterparts in advantaged neighbourhoods (Acheson, 1998). By observation to date, corona-virus has a large impact in polarising society; it plays a position in making differences greater, in both the realm of health and economy.

The more we can increase the breadth of positive experiences across the lifespan, accessible to all, the more we seek to reduce vulnerabilities. Typically, barriers to engagement with activities include cost, availability, access difficulties, or thinking that the activity is 'not for them'. It is suggested that increasing participation in positive activities, such as yoga, may support people to broaden their experience, develop their interests and support positive mental health and emotional wellbeing.

On a community level, increasing opportunities for yoga, especially online, either for free or an affordable cost has the potential to create more cohesive and resilient communities with values of diversity and difference. Sharing yoga as accessible for all can help people to develop resilience and wider social and emotional skills and be physically, mentally emotionally healthy.

Empowering people to try out new ideas and activities such as yoga may diversify their experience of what supports them to feel more mentally and physically well, as well as empower them to connect with something less conventional than talking therapies.

In this period of social distancing and real-life disconnect, yoga can be viewed as a means of bringing people together, to form new relationships with others that they may otherwise not have met, as well as experience a sense of belonging as part of a new community. The elements of fun and enjoyment that yoga offers enables a shared experience of shared connection, beyond diversity and difference, that further serves to promote positive health.

7. Moving Forward To 'Come Back Home'

'In the waves of change, we find our true direction'

We are living in a time of discomfort, distress and dis-ease; and as Martin Luther King, Jr. reminded us, *'the ultimate measure of man is not where he stands in moments of comfort and convenience'*. We are all adjusting to sitting with uncertainty and tolerating distress. Almost the work of a whole therapy journey, yet we are being forced into learning the 'how' with our own creative therapeutic ways at home. Yoga can be your own therapeutic tool. Yoga is not a spiritual bypass, and there is no requirement of a faith or religion, it is a journey inwards, to your own inner world. Yoga offers itself to a path of inner healing, seeking to soothe and stabilise what's going on internally, whilst trying to understand the larger meanings beyond. As Stephen Cope (2018) advocates, *'our task is not to free ourselves from the world but to fully embrace the world, to embrace the real'*.

Mahatma Ghandi encouraged us to 'grow and evolve'. We are being called to grow and evolve individually, socially and globally at a very rapid rate, from an incredibly powerful and unexpected curve ball. Yoga teacher BKS Iyengar claimed that *'change is not something we should fear. Rather, it is something that we should welcome. For without change, nothing in this world would ever grow or blossom, and no one in this world would ever move forward to become the person they're meant to be'*.

Given that awareness is the greatest agent for change, yoga supports us with the internal awareness required for change to occur, scaffolding the process of growth and transformation to direct the journey of healing.

There are many lessons that we may learn from Alice of Alice in Wonderland, let this be one. When Alice starts to question who she is, how she should live, and what is her place in the world, she reflects, *'It's no use going back to yesterday because I was a different person then'*. Every day we grow and change, every nugget of experience shapes and guides our inner thoughts, feelings, behaviours and physical body, and impacts our interactions with ourselves, others and the world around us. Our experiences lend to the stories we tell and how we make sense of what we have lived through. As the thoughts we have and words we speak have power, encourage your stories to be one of strength, resilience and growth.

Given that the now is the only real living moment, let it be one that does not cling onto what has already gone, yet invests in a brighter one for what arrives next. As C. S. Lewis inspires, *'there are better things ahead than any we leave behind'*.

Please know there is hope. In the previous months that have passed, aspects of life that were once unimaginable have unfolded before our eyes and re-shaped our daily lives. However, amongst all that we have bared witness to, we have also been gifted with positives that did not seem possible. More time families and getting to know our own children, re-juggling working life to transport our work remotely like a digital nomad escaping the office, a vast reconsideration of policies and practices, the weekly community clap for key workers that lifts the neighbourhood spirits, the doorstep dining's and stoop-side hangs with friends, the long, long walks and mother nature healing herself against global warming.... The things that we would never have made time for, and now seem a small luxury. Have hope and believe that positive change is possible; this hope starts at home, it starts within, it starts with you.

There is no home greater than your own, yourself. Yoga is the practice of coming back home.

Dr Stephanie Minchin

About The Author

Dr Stephanie Minchin (@theyogapsychologist) is a Clinical Psychologist and Yoga Teacher with complimentary advanced training in Yoga Therapy.

In her practice as a Clinical Psychologist, Stephanie works with children, adolescents and young people in mental health services in East London offering individual and group psychological therapy, as well as consultation to education and social care systems. Stephanie believes in looking beyond the power of diagnostic labels and contextualises difficulties to life experiences unique to the individual, working from a positive psychology perspective for strength and growth to overcome adversity.

As Stephanie furthered her training as a Yoga Teacher, she realised that the parallel between sharing psychological therapy and yoga classes was about 'holding space' for others and inviting inner connection to understand oneself. In the discovery of yoga therapy, Stephanie pursued further training with The Minded Institute to compliment her passions and interests in yoga and psychology, uniting the two disciplines in a more holistic approach.

Yoga has become not only a regular feature of Stephanie's daily practice and routine, yet also an integral part of her life as a way of living. Yoga has supported Stephanie to become more grounded, mindful and self-compassionate, with an approach of acceptance and gratitude each day. Stephanie advocates that yoga isn't about just making shapes on the mat, yet is a journey of inner self-awareness with self-inquiry. Stephanie believes that there is an offering of yoga for everybody and everybody, with its gifts having transformative and healing powers.

Stephanie regularly teaches community yoga classes with MoreYoga, and co-founded the MoreMind project, raising awareness of mental health through yoga. Stephanie writes articles and runs monthly workshops integrating yoga and psychology to enhance mental wellbeing and emotional resilience.

Contact Dr Stephanie Minchin (@theyogapsychologist)

theyogapsychologist@gmail.com for Psychological Therapy, 1:1 Yoga, Yoga Therapy

In Captivity & Isolation, We Found Freedom

The strange times we are in now are speculated to be because of many things... 5G Related, Biological war, and many other theories lie behind this global crisis we as human beings now find ourselves in. However it got here, we are all now very much in it and affected by it. Months in lock down, and the government have put us all under house arrest for the good of all, to protect the vulnerable. There is to be no school, no commute to work, no clubs, not even free for all at the shops, no nothing. Stay in your homes and in your gardens, with your family.

When historians tell of this time, which they will of course and the people read about our situation and our freedoms taken away, what will they think? I believe they will think, this was the beginning of the great awakening, this was the catalyst for change, this was the time in history when the human being remembered who they were and what they were; free from labels, student, manager, businessman or otherwise, when the human being realised that they had been living in captivity since the day they were born in to the system. They were born in to a nation of human doings not beings and the Earth allowed a virus to help them wake up and see, how little freedom they have and yet how much they can have, if they just take their personal power back.

You Have Been Given The Luxury Of Time

In captivity/isolation the people could breathe. They were present with the ones they love whether they lived together or apart, they become conscious. They planted food, they checked on strangers and neighbours they stopped polluting their world and their souls.

In our everyday lives we trade time with ourselves and our loved ones for money so we can buy food, pay for water and power and a roof over our head; but not just that, the latest phone, gadget, handbag etc. We have become a very excess oriented society. The society of not enough and I must have bigger and better has wreaked havoc in our relationships with ourselves and each other, the mental health of not just adults but children.

We have depleted our nature and nature around us on a catastrophic level. We have tipped the balance and it has not gone in the favour of our emotional, mental or physical wellbeing

This is our time now human beings. How can you stay sane and mentally healthy at this time of perceived lack of freedom? Put simply, remember who you are. Remember who you were before the world told you who you are and what you must do. Spiritual beings having a human experience with more power than you can imagine as an individual and collectively.

Right now, is our opportunity for spiritual and personal growth and rest and repair. Yes there is much uncertainty for many of us and for the world, but we are more than a number in our bank as much as we are more than a number on the scales and for the first time the system has been forced in to closure, giving us time to wake up and be the change we want to see in our personal lives and in our collective consciousness.

So, what can we do? Well firstly let us get over the guilt at doing nothing, this is all part of the human doing sickness we are so heavily indoctrinated in. Just do nothing, be nothing but you and then begin to start the very overdue conversation with yourself.

The sheer magnitude of all that is happening is overwhelming, all change starts from one act and a ripple effect that follows, that is how the Corona virus exists and that is how any virus or trouble begins is with one action. It is also the same for the good things that come, it all comes from one action, the good comes from the human spirit being strong in its power to create change, stand up for what is right and true and right now the focus is on YOU, YOU are superhero of this story. It is time to ask yourself some questions that can, if you wish change your life.

Being able to bring about change first requires the time to acknowledge that you need or want it. This is the gift in the crisis. A time of reflection before the human doing machine finds the reboot button and wants you to go back to business as usual against your souls yearning.

We only have one thing we must do on this planet and that is to be who we truly are, which is love. WE must be and do love in every word and action, this is our place of indestructible power.

When we are who we want to be and we do what our soul intended us to do, our heart is happy our stress levels reduced. We are at peace with ourselves as we are not resisting our true essence, the essence of who we are paves the way for our own wonderful life, which in turn touches others and inspires and motivates them to do the same.

Use this precious gift of time to ask yourself reflective questions. Spend time alone at night or day depending on your household and its noise levels. (I am a mum of 6 so I grab before they get up or in the middle of the night). In the quiet, in the stillness, breathe deep, and have this intimate conversation with yourself. The only real conversation that matters is the one no one teaches us to have until we have traded so much of our essence, so much of our time and happiness that we are too far down the rabbit hole to notice that we have just been coasting in someone else's story, too powerless and distracted to step in to our own.

Intimate conversations require an intimate setting, so if you are not sure how to hear your hearts voice in your head, I suggest you set the stage. To get the best results you must limit to eliminate toxins.

Imagine you are preparing for one of the most important conversations of your life, be it career or relationship related, you wouldn't go in intoxicated and unprepared you would be ready, clear head, on a mission to pursue or accept big changes, strong of body and mind, calm and collected.

Suggested Actions To Take:

- Avoid Caffeine – It is an unnecessary stimulant that goes against being calm and open, interrupts natural sleep patterns and can cause you to feel anxious, taking you out of the relaxed rest and repair state that we need to stay in for our task.
- Choose herbal teas, hot lemon water - Any drink that hydrates the cells of the body rather than ask it to do extra work.
- Don't eat a huge stodgy meal or big take away then go and try and create this conversation. You could feel physically fatigued and potentially have a sluggish negative mind-set.
- Avoid Sugar – The sugar blues is a real thing, when we want to connect with our highest self, we need to leave the self-sabotaging, toxic, stimulating factors at the door.
- Eat a diet high in plant-based foods. All food has a vibration; natural, organic plant-based foods provide our body and mind the highest vibrational fuel for the healthiest body and mind. The more

- open and calm the body is the more receptive the heart mind connection and the clearer the communication.
- Include Superfoods. Superfoods are always good, named that way as they provide you so much, it is a subject matter in itself but when your body receives nutrient dense, high vibrational foods your stress levels are reduced, your happiness comes easier and your immune system stays strong in defence. I currently would recommend a spoonful of spirulina a day in some fresh orange juice or a well-balanced smoothie. Its ability to heighten you on both physical and spiritual level is never more so important as it is now.
- Spend time in the fresh air, this may be from your balcony, window, garden or a local quiet walk anywhere you are isolated for the reasons of the global pandemic but also so you can make space for your spirit to talk to you and so you have to time to reflect on all you have to be grateful for in the world of never ending abundance.

The above recommendations are not essential for the conversation with self but will help you get the best results; a polluted body is a polluted mind so, a well-nourished and nurtured body will give you a clear, healthy mind.

Set The Stage By Creating A Mini Ritual:

Essential Tools:

Pen and Journal - For me, my journal is a conversation with myself and makes sense and silence out of the mental madness my mind likes to try and inflict on me.

Optional Extras And Highly Recommend:

Essential Oils Or Incense:

A great one for meditation is frankincense. It is of course the king of oils and hey it if is good enough for Jesus it is good enough for us, right? Frankincense is so high vibrational; it literally raises your cellular health. This means it is great for immunity as well as fighting depression it calms the mind soothe our fears, and works on the pineal gland which is what the ancients documented as being the window, not just to our soul but to the universe itself.

You may need some meditation music or just your favourite tunes that help ground you and any racing thoughts. Breathing deeply, slowly relaxes your whole body, making it easier to connect with

your mind, heart and soul. I personally like the alternate nostril breathing, there are many advantageous ways to breathe to relax body and mind and I encourage you to find the one that works best for you. The only important 'MUST DO' about this conversation is having it openly and honestly and making it happen.

Start This Very Important Conversation With The Suggested Following Questions:

Q. How do you normally spend your time? Does it make you happy? If not, why? How would you like to spend your time? Can you do that now, or can you see how you can make it possible?

Q. What value do I add to the lives of others?

Q. Do I practice self-care? Do I look after myself like I do those I love? If not, how can you start doing this?

Q. How reliant am I on a system to provide for my basic needs of food and hydration? Can I become more self-sufficient? What steps can I take to be able to provide for my basic needs and that of those I love?

Q. What are you passionate about? Have you forgotten what you're passionate about? Do you do or have what you are passionate about? If now how can you change this?

Q What would happen if I do not be who I am and pursue things I truly love? What will my life legacy be?

Q. Am I kind? Am I caring?

Q. Do you value your physical body, which is the vehicle for your soul's life purpose, or do you find you ask too much of it and need to give back.

Q. Do you like what you see? Are you happy? Is there anything you wish was different?

There is no limit to the questions you can ask, it is your conversation. These are helpful suggestions to use this crisis as a gift to *'know thyself'*. Know that you are important, you are worthy of all the happiness you crave and deserve. Nothing is too big a leap if it is your hearts calling, help yourself and help your fellow human and together in our awakened consciousness we can help give back to the earth that we have ravaged so fiercely over the past 60 years.

Remember we are all as one, all part of the cosmos, all crucial and essential. We matter, what we do or do not do matters. Chose this gift of time to remember who you are and be that human. Life and the world we are part of is more wonderful than you have been able to see. Now is your time, now is our time, the time of the rise of the Human being and the fall of the human doing and the powers that enforce this outdated system of take more than you give.

WAKE UP, YOU HAVE TIME, BE THE CHANGE,

WE ARE ONE, WE ARE LOVE, ONLY LOVE IS REAL

Knowing yourself is the beginning of all wisdom - Aristotle

Rebecca McQueen

About The Author

I am a proud mother to 6 wonderful children and a health coach who has 10 professional years helping people with both their physical and emotional well-being.

I suffered with anxiety and depression from a very young age which was the driving force behind my passion for self-discovery and wellness.

Years later I made my passion and purpose my profession and have had the privilege of helping others rediscover who they are, align with their purpose and look after their body and mind.

I love what I do, I love people, the planet and the journey.

https://www.stresslesshealthcoach.co.uk/

Stuck At Home? From Overwhelmed & Stressed To Engaged & Connected

Abstract - The challenges of being stuck at home with everyone... "From overwhelmed & stressed to engaged and connected". To helping the whole family get along better. A Psychologists perspective on improving family dynamics... The strength of the parent-child relationship and the cohesiveness of the couple relationship - both in intimacy and in shared parenting. This chapter considers some of the challenges and offers practical suggestions for improving things together at home.

A worldwide health crisis has turned 2020 into a year that no-one expected. A year that will certainly be remembered for a very long time. From stability to destabilisation. From normality to - ??? All we hear about on the news is about Corona virus. Nearly everything we hear when conversing with others is about Covid 19... Facebook, news, papers... This issue has given many people changes and challenges. There are significant mandatory rules in each country – isolated from family, from friends, and often workplaces... The situation has so many widespread impacts and ramifications. Some people say to "find the opportunities and positives", but for others this will be the challenge. Some will experience fear, anxiety and paranoia, while others will re-focus, re-engage and increase their resilience. Where will you be?

This chapter will consider the home environment. It is a Psychologists perspective on how to improve your wellbeing during this time. We will consider how you and your family can not only survive, but "thrive". This chapter will look at how you can move from feeling overwhelmed and stressed, to engaged and connected. We will examine some alternative ways of thinking and some strategies that will assist you at this time.

The Areas Covered Include:

- Family Interactions/Dynamics

- Self-Care

- Child Interactions

- Parent-Child Relationships

- Couple Relationships

Around the world, Psychologists are known for their skills and expertise. As mental health professionals, Psychologists can assist in a range of ways – this can include consulting with Government and organisations, to providing counselling or therapy. Some Psychologists are involved in creating policy or developing resources for the public. In these challenging times, many people access the internet for resources, support or information. As a Psychologist, I contribute in writing (blogs, book chapters, e-books), in presentations (at Conferences or to the general public), in training new Psychologists and in consulting directly with people (face to face or online/telehealth). **As A Psychologist My Passion Is All Aspects Of Wellbeing And Helping To Improve Life!**

The situation itself is a significant trigger for many people. A trigger of anxiety, fear and emotional disturbance. Some people in the community are worried, really worried about their own health, or about the health of their loved ones. This worry can be real or it can be escalating anxiety. For some people there is a fear, even a paranoia about the illness and what could happen. Some people are acting irrationally or being offensive in their interactions with others. These attitudes and behaviour leads to other actions and behaviours – some people are therefore "self-isolating" to protect themselves and their family, other people are "self-isolating" to protect community members who may be vulnerable. Each country around the world has a different rule or requirement at different times right now. What we need to remember is the importance of RESPECT in all of this. It is a challenging time but all of us have individual responsibility.

Family Interactions

Spending time together is great – right? There are so many things we can do. For some families, being together is fun and enjoyable. For other families, it is stressful, distressing, boring or even conflictual. For some people – the holidays are a "breeze", while for others it is a huge challenge. So when the country changes the rules – and there are people being isolated, and when things are cancelled and changed or don't happen. This is a big surprise, a challenge or even distressful.

We know that children gain comfort and security from routines as well as a range of things in their life. (Adults too can find that routines and regularity provide stability and consistency). For children, this can involve a positive relationship with their parents and a consistent routine. When parents understand their child (and their emotions) then the child is better able to be free to share their emotions.

The majority of people would be aware that stress impacts on our functioning, and on our immune system. It impacts on our sleep, our emotion management, and our interactions with others. So, spending time with others can be great, or it can be distressing. Everyone's tolerance is different, and interactions in our family and community impact on our mental health and daily functioning.

Being isolated can be a particular challenge. So also, can being stuck in a small space with the same people for a period of time. It will be important for parents and families to closely monitor their mood and interactions.

Parents are the role models for children. Children are watching – watching how their parents deal with emotions, or conflict, interactions with others or even themselves. So, as children grow, they learn to make choices and to experience responsibility and consequences. Parents are there to guide and assist children, and the strength of the parent- child relationship is most important. Have a think about how your parent-child relationship is going and what could be different.

A Few Strategies To Assist:

••☐ Having some fun things to do together. Board games. Listening to music. Gardening.

••☐ Having some time apart – doing what each of us are interested in. Reading a book, going to the park. Listening to music or drawing.

••☐ Maintaining consistency with routines is important – eating, breaks, sleeping.

- Engaging with a counsellor or Psychologist to provide support for managing emotions or for parenting and relationship support. This can be face to face or telehealth. Many counsellors and Psychologists are providing online sessions at this time.

Is Home Schooling Driving You Nuts?

Suddenly found yourself stuck at home with the kids? All over our country, indeed, around the world – Schools maybe been shut down by the Government, and there are so many changes in our world. Staying home can be a challenge for many people – particularly if there are a few kids in the mix. Its sometimes a challenge when everyone is home on the holidays – but this is everyone home, for a much longer time AND to do school work. So you are all stuck at home together – everyday! So it's not unusual for parents to be feeling like they are "nuts" or "losing it" or that things can get out of control. You didn't train to be a "teacher", right? This could be even tougher than usual parenting. Change can be hard for everyone to deal with and we have some things that will help.

Managing Kids' Emotions

It can be a challenge for kids on a number of levels – change, emotions, siblings, home environment instead of school Now they've got mum or dad telling them what to do all day – that could be tough. Some kids manage their emotions well and others can be easily triggered into meltdown with changes, with no familiar school environment, with siblings nearby, with the struggles of a parent in a different role.

So Here Are A Few Tips To Help Your Kids:

1	Set out a clear visual structure with regular activity breaks.
2	Give kids a choice on what to do e.g. – would you like to do maths or spelling first.
3Have time together to do some fun things – this will help with improving your relationship and connection.
4Allow children some time to express emotions & energy (trampoline, kick a ball around).

Helping Parents To Cope:

Many parents are struggling with the changes too. If everyone is together in the same space for all day and every day, for days on end that can be tough. Ok – it might feel like you are "going nuts!" but you're not the only one - chances are, everyone else is feeling like that too.

Here Are Some Things To Help:

1	Get a good night's sleep (if that's hard, seek professional advice!).
2	Have some regular alone time (go for a walk in the garden or to the park).
3	Have someone you can debrief with (partner, friend, parent or professional).

Being home with your child – or all your kids can be challenging. Home schooling can be very different. There is a way to get through this and still enjoy life! You can survive! You will survive! Implement these family friendly strategies and find some things you can enjoy doing together – not only at the end of the day but during the day as well.

If things continue to be challenging – contact a Psychologist for a confidential consultation. We can provide parenting advice, information or counselling. You can receive counselling for parents or children – spending time with a professional can assist in better understanding your body and emotions.

Self-Care

Looking after yourself when "stuck at home" could be a challenge for many people. Some people live by themselves and like to be alone others may live by themselves and thrive on being social and interacting with a range of people. Others are by themselves but already have anxieties, depression or other mental health challenges to manage.

Some people live with a partner or family – but still, the challenges of self-care are relevant. Many people participate in team sports (can't do that now) or in catching up with friends (certainly not allowed in many countries). Some people find purpose and meaning in their work or in the community (volunteering or personal projects). All of this is now reduced or removed, which means that many people are now at home in the same space as all their family.

It's important first to be aware of how you are going. That involves some self-awareness and some self-reflection. Managing your emotions and managing your responses and your interactions with others. Many people find that physical activity can assist in their overall wellbeing, but also in their emotion management. Being able to spend some time in nature will greatly assist, but if you can't be outside, then listen to some relaxing music, maybe even some active music – and find some form of physical activity that will work for you. Some people like gym, others enjoy yoga, while others need to ride a bike, walk or swim.

Here's Some Things To Help:

1   Participate in physical activity.
2   Have a goal or a project to get involved in.
3   Listen to some music.
4Do something that is relaxing for you (bath, cook, read a book, sit in the sun, garden).

Children & Child Interactions:

Each child is different and will experience things differently. A child who usually copes with life "fine" may still be "fine" or they may decline. As outlined earlier though, "change" can create another "change" and so as a parent "be aware" and "be alert" as things may be challenging for a while. It may be your child usually copes well with the routine and structure of life and now, things are different. It may be that your child is struggling with not playing with or seeing their friends. Maybe the home isolation is confronting, all that news on the virus and the people dying and their own anxiety has increased. Or perhaps, it's all your children just annoying each other, being in each other's personal space, and pushing the "buttons"!

Some Considerations For What May Assist:

1   Your child will need some alone time too...

2. Helping your child manage their emotions, reflecting their feelings, showing that you understand.
3. Physical activity is great for assisting with emotion management.
4. Check out some great websites.

Parent-Child Relationships:

Over the years, I have seen and heard many parents share their difficulties, concerns and challenges. The biggest concerns that parents have are often around children and their emotions. This often looks like tantrums, "losing it" and "meltdowns". Sometimes, this situation is related to other developmental challenges, sensory sensitivities or complex considerations like Autism. However, depending on their age, many children do actually have control over their emotions. It may just be that the situation has triggered them very fast into overwhelm or emotional overload.

Sometimes children have some low level anxiety – basically they are worried about something. Sometimes it is "change" and sometimes it is a situation that has occurred before – something that previously was stressful or distressing. For some children it is new things, or things that are out of their routine. For other children it is a situation where their brain is thinking, over thinking or needing many small, minor details resolved. This brain activity may cause their body to experience a range of emotions that are difficult to manage. Some children are not aware of their thought processes, just the feelings in their body. So everyone is different and experiences life differently.

The First Thing That Parents Can Do To Help Their Children With Behaviour, Is To Help Children With Their Feelings. This Can Happen In A Few Ways. Most Importantly, For The Parent To Acknowledge The Child's Feelings. For Example, "Johnny, I Can See That You Are Upset" Or "Mary, You Look Like That Is Frustrating You". This Helps A Child See That You Are Noticing Their Feelings, And Interested In Them. If Your Child Thinks You Go The "Feeling" That You Identified As "Wrong" Then I Am Sure That They Will Let You Know – And You Can Then Respond; "Oh, Ahh You Are Feeling Annoyed - Not Angry". Again, This Helps The Child See That You Are Noticing Their Feelings And That They Are Being Focused On.

A Second key strategy is to spend one on one time with your child. Many parents think that they have a good relationship with their child, but often don't realise that this relationship is often on specific terms and with a specific focus. Many parents and children benefit from having some "special time" together each week. For example, half an hour together – where the child decides the activity and the parent is responsive. For example, instead of the parent suggesting activity or playing the way that "they" want to then in this specific activity the child takes the lead and the parent is respectful of this and lets the child "lead". In some therapeutic techniques this is often referred to as "Special Time" within Filial Therapy or child-parent relationship therapy. A number of professionals are able to provide Parent skills training in techniques that assist the parent to be more responsive and attuned in their relationship.

Another strategy for helping children, involves the parent having a consistent routine and clear boundaries. It's important for children to feel safe and secure and a regular routine will assist with that. It may be more challenging for children (if their parents are separated), for the child/children to have a routine across both care environments. But it can be done, particularly when parents are able to communicate respectfully together and to collaborate with their ex-partner. Many children have difficulty concentrating at school, or difficulty managing their emotions, simply because they are tired or overtired. It is important for everyone in the family to have a good nights' sleep.

It is important for children and their parents to respect and care for each other. Being able to communicate feelings is essential in any relationship.

Couple Relationships
Being in a relationship can have its challenges. There are many people who will be happy in their relationship, but this widespread change may even rock their boat. A change in one aspect of our life, can impact in other areas. Some couples maybe in a good routine, and this situation can change things for them. Maybe the time together balance is great, but

now you have to be together all day, every day and that's tough. Maybe you need your space, your individual time. Maybe you each need social time and can't get it now. So many things that are now different.

Some couples will have challenges that are broader and far reaching. One partner or both may lose their job. This can add extra stress and difficulties. Perhaps one partner now needs to give up their job to be responsible for providing supervision or schooling for the child/children. This can create extra strain and additional challenges. For others, the changes can be more positive – allowing them time they don't usually have. A forced "slow-down" can have some beneficial side effects – more time together, more relaxing and more togetherness.

Ultimately your partner needs you to care for them, and respect them. Allowing them to meet their individual needs will assist in the relational aspects. Taking it easy on each other – being more supportive and understanding in these challenging times.

A Few Things That Can Assist Include:

1. Having some time together separate to the children (maybe in means taking turns for "my time" and allowing your partner to rejuvenate or recuperate).
2. Arranging a date night – in-house- but something special!
3. Find out about "the 5 love languages" and do the quiz...

Your well-being during the corona virus is important. You are a part of a family, a community, a country, a world. Being connected is important. Engaging with your friends and family, in whatever ways are allowable and appropriate for where you are living right now.

Make some conscious decisions to move from the stress and overwhelmed bubble – and head on over to the engaged and connected sphere.

There are many challenges and I hope that this information has been helpful.

Jay Anderson

About The Author

Jay is a Psychologist, Coach and Counsellor. She has over 25 year's experience in helping people with a range of challenges. Jay lives in southwest Western Australia - engaging with clients online and in person at the Southwest Wellbeing Centre. Jay's passion is "making a difference" and she is excited to be a part of this important project.

To find out more you will find Jay at:

Website: http://www.swwellbeing.com.au

If you would like to join our mailing list or receive a free e-book on Better understanding your well-being, then I can be contacted for more information on info@swwellbeing.com.au

Recommended Resources:

Gary Chapman-1992:

The Five Love Languages: How to Express Heartfelt Commitment to Your Mate

Gary Chapman and Ross Campbell 2016:

The Five Love Languages Of Children

Hand in Hand Parenting.org.

Stan Ferguson 2010:

The 5 Key Steps To Stay Happy And Healthy Whilst Running Your Business From Home

Running your business is stressful at the best of times but working from home, alongside children (even the four legged kind), partners, house work, home schooling and distractions can compound the pressure considerably. Throw in a Global Pandemic and it takes the stress to a whole new level.

It sounds easy in theory; wake up ... walk to your home desk and get lots of work done building your empire and fulfilling your purpose to make the world a better place doing what you love. However, for many the opposite is true and it can involve a lot of stopping and starting, unfinished to do lists and a sense of cabin fever like no other.

I am pleased to confirm that the former can be your reality. You can work effectively from home (even around children), get lots done and not feel like the walls are closing in on you on a daily basis.

As a coach who has worked from home since the birth of my son almost three years ago, I understand the trials and tribulations of working from home and ensuring that it becomes a happy and productive workplace that complements your family life. As the 'hub' of your global empire you join many amazing entrepreneurs who have built a business from their kitchen table including Jo Malone, and Sophia Amoruso.

**Here Are My 5 Key Steps
To Stay Happy And Healthy Whilst Running Your Business From Home:**

Step 1: Embrace Your Reality

I'll never forget my first day running my business from home; my son was just a week old and asleep in one arm and I had about two hours in between feeds to get some work done. I opened my laptop on my table, started to write a newsletter one handed and immediately started to cry. I couldn't believe that this was now my 'office'. Having spent years in the corporate world with a dedicated workspace, time to myself to get everything done and colleagues to chat to; I felt alone, afraid and not sure what to do next.

After a good cry to myself (and lots of newborn cuddles), I decided to just go easy on myself and accept my reality. If I wanted to build a business around my son then my working life would never be the same again and I would have to work from home.

So, I started to see things differently and remind myself how lucky I was to work from home and never waste time with a commute, Starbucks queues and forgetting my computer password. Over time it became my reality and I now love working from home. Whether this is a short term situation for you and something more long term; embrace it. What you resist persists and if you have any resentment towards working from home, you will feel the impact of this quickly.

Fall in love with the fact that you GET to work from home and the more time this will give you on a daily basis. Fall in love with the fact that you are in control and, regardless of the distractions at home, you are the creator of your work life balance.

Step 2: Create The Right Environment:

After my first attempt at writing a newsletter, with my son in my arms and tears in my eyes, I realised I had to create the right working environment for me. Realistically I could only hold my son in my arms for so long before it became uncomfortable so I invested in an Ipad (to work on when he was asleep on me and / or feeding) and a sling (so I could pop him in there when asleep and sit at my table and work with two hands). Both came in very handy and helped me create the right environment at that time.

Now my environment consists of a desk, wall of success (I'll discuss below), laptop and enough stationery to start my own shop. If you are to run your business from home, then you need a dedicated space within your home to work from. This can be the kitchen table, a desk in your bedroom or a home office. What matters is that when you sit down to work; YOU FEEL LIKE YOU'RE AT WORK and you have everything you need at your fingertips. Ensure this workspace has limited distractions (I usually find having my back to the dishes works) and that you can dedicate your time to running your business.

If a set space within your home is prime real estate and just not possible to solely dedicate as your work space then perhaps a really nice box that you can pop your laptop, paperwork and anything else you need to run your business in once you are finished working for the day and free up your 'office' space for other activities like dinner, arts and crafts and family games.

One of my clients, Claudia, is a mum of three teenage boys and has no set space to work from home as she balances home schooling and a husband who permanently works from home. Unable to pop to a local coffee shop to work she has a beautiful bag that holds her laptop, notebooks and pens and she neatly packs it up after work and moves it from room to room depending on where her office will be that day.

Having your own work space allows you the opportunity to 'transition' from home life to work life and feel like a proper business owner. This has a positive knock on effect on your mind-set and allows you to get into business owner mode and create the results you desire.

** Top Tip: In my home office I also have a WALL OFF SUCCESS where I have a single wall dedicated to my goals for the next year. Here I have a vision board with my annual goals, and then charts showing my plan for the next 12 weeks to help me achieve these goals.

When you write out your goals; you are much more likely to achieve them. Imagine then how successful you and your business can be if you have your goals right in front of you and you can see them every day. This has been one of the most powerful steps in helping me achieve success in business. If you have kids; consider getting them involved in creating their goals and creating a vision board they can share and look at their goals daily.

My friend Gemma and I took her twin 12 year old daughters out for lunch where we all created our vision board and they popped theirs on their wall of success. Children need motivation too and how lovely is it for them to look at their goals during lockdown.

Step 3. Be Your Own Leader

When I first worked from home, I was easily distracted (and I don't just mean by my new born baby). There was always a new TV shows, a magazine to read, housework to complete and of course something to distract me on social media. It really took a few months for the penny to drop and for me to realise that there was no one coming to check on me and ensure that I got everything done. I didn't have a manager to report to, weekly opps meetings to attend and no longer pitched at monthly KPI meetings. This was a huge adjustment for me.

One day, I navigated a trip to Starbucks and sat down and wrote out all the ways I distracted myself and failed to commit to growing my business. When you work for yourself; there is a lot of pressure, from building a strong and committed customer base to how you position yourself online, the pressure can seem endless. So, I decided there and then that I would not add to this pressure and commit to becoming the leader I always wished I had when I was in the corporate world.

This was such a beautiful opportunity for me. No longer would I complain about my manager not understanding me and how I worked as I decided to become the leader that was perfect for me. One that was committed to my vision, acknowledged me when I did well and challenged me when I could do better. This leader ROCKED!

Immediately I started to set 12 week goals (that fitted into my yearly vision) and plan a weekly 'CEO' meeting with myself where I would:

- Assess my 12 week goals and ensure I was still emotionally connected to them (and add them to my wall of success).
- Assess the work I had completed over the past week and give myself praise when I achieved everything and compassion when I didn't and
- Set goals for the week ahead.

Over time, I went one step further and I committed to 'owning my day' and setting clear tasks that I wanted to achieve that day. Gone were the lists with 100 things to do and these were replaced by three key tasks that when completed would make a massive difference to whether or not I achieved my goals. I spent time setting up systems for things that were taking up my time on a consistent basis and also outsourced tasks that could be done to a high standard and faster by someone else.

Regularly I set 'power hours' where I pop on some motivating music (or glorious silence) and commit to solely focusing on one task until it is complete. The feeling at the end of one hour is amazing and totally spurs me on to get more work done afterwards. I would 'reward' myself after one hour and look forward to my green teas, quick shot of social media or a cheeky piece of chocolate.

One of my friends Lesley is a mum of two and has to lead herself and her children when working from home. She has identified when her family works best and runs her online classes Monday, Tuesday, Wednesday and home-schools her girls the rest of the week. Part of her leadership style is identifying the 'rhythm' of her family and when she needs to be mum and when she needs to be a business owner. Rather than time blocking her day … she looks at her week and goes from there. She also allows time at night to catch up on admin work for her business.

Only one person will lead you to success when working from home … and that's you! Identify the leader you would love to have and go and become that person. How committed is this leader? How inspiring are they? How compassionate are they? Write out all the attributes of the leader you want to become and go and become her.

And ensure that the leader you become has a clear plan for success. Create a sacred time every week to hold a CEO meeting with yourself and hold yourself accountable for all the amazing goals you want to achieve. But most importantly, understand that what works for others may not work for you and your household. Stand tall and embrace that you can choose how and when you work and celebrate this.

** Top Tip: Make your weekly CEO meeting super special. Cook yourself your favourite meal, grab your favourite drink or do whatever you want to make it special. This time represents you and your commitment to your business growth and deserves to be special.

Step 4: Stay Connected And Build Your Tribe

The truth is that running your business from home can be lonely. Loneliness set in for me by about week two of being my own boss. By then I had spent 7 days alone with my baby while my then partner had gone back to work and felt lost, confused and wondering what to do next.

Like many women, I created an online Facebook community for mums in business and started to run child friendly networking events in my local City. Within a couple of hours of setting up the Facebook community I had about 200 women join and could instantly connect with them, share challenges and get advice and much needed support. This community kept growing and kept me sane when running my business from home and the networking events gave me something to look forward to. During Covid-19 I switched to running online networking events so we could continue to keep the connection going.

Social Connection during the current climate is essential. The wonderful thing is that there are so many online 'tribes' available to join and if you don't find one you like; you can create one of your own. Make it the perfect one just for you and offering exactly what you need.

Your tribe can grow as you and your business do and as time progressed I also partnered with an accountability partner to both help me achieve my goals and to share my challenges and successes with. This helped immensely in staying happy and healthy and I looked forward to our weekly coffees and virtual catch ups. Knowing someone else believes in your goals makes a huge difference in your ability to achieve them.

How Can You Stay Connected While Running Your Business From Home?

How can you build (or join) a tribe of like-minded people online (or take your offline community online)?

Can you find an accountability partner to support you on this journey?

** Top Tip: Join a few communities and see what works best for you. You may not get all you need and want from just one so engage in a few and see what happens.

Step 5: Live Your Life To The Fullest:

Sitting eating my third chocolate bar of the day with a sleeping baby beside me and I started to get this strange feeling that there had to be more to life. I seemed to spend all day every day nursing or cuddling a baby or working; with little in between including sleep.

It felt like Groundhog Day and I was really starting to question my decision and this feeling has been recreated during lockdown. Sometimes it seems like you're living the same day every day and this can bring up mixed emotions. Boredom, frustration, contentment, happiness and everything in between.

I found giving myself something to look forward to while working from home is essential. Scheduling in 'rewards' that excited me has been a key driver in keeping me happy and healthy whilst running my business from home.

Make a list of all the 'rewards' you can create whilst working from home and schedule them in. Perhaps you want a new book and some time to read this ... what milestone will you reach whereby you will reward yourself with this? Plan that milestone into your weekly goals and then some time to enjoy your reward.

Perhaps you want a new laptop/ coffee maker / notebook etc. Whatever your 'reward' is, just make sure it inspires you to take action and gives you something to look forward to. Your reward doesn't have to be something you 'purchase'; it can be a lunch out with your friends, a skype call with a mentor, time to meditate, or WHATEVER YOU WANT IT TO BE. Ensure it is a reward and not a coping mechanism (hello eating too much chocolate) and not something that is a short term high and a long term low.

Ask yourself regularly; Why did you start your own business? What type of life did you want it to provide for you?

Your business is only one part of your amazing life and so often the temptation is to 'hustle' and 'slay' and lose yourself in the process. Poor boundaries when working from home can mean you constantly have one eye on the phone even when you're supposed to be with your kids / partner / even meditating.

Set goals in all areas of your life. Those goals that really light you up and make you really feel alive. Book that massage, enrol in that class, learn that new skill and go on that holiday. Live your life your way and ensure it is rich and full in all areas with a business that helps you achieve this. You are an incredible human being and there is only one of you in the world. Go be YOU!

It is possible to run a business from home and stay happy and healthy. You can build the business of your dreams from your kitchen table, become so productive that achieving your goals seems easy whilst building your tribe and living a fulfilled life. It doesn't have to be scary ... it just takes a new level of awareness and a commitment to make this work.

Orlaith Brogan

About The Author

One-to-one life and business coaching - helping women to become the best versions of themselves

Orlaith Brogan takes a no-nonsense approach to shifting mind-sets, breaking internal barriers and supporting women across the UK to realise their full potential.

Two years ago, Orlaith Brogan decided that it was time to make a change, not only for herself, but also for other like-minded mums across the UK facing the same dilemmas as her. Shifting her own mindset and realising that she was in fact worthy, she set out on an entrepreneurial path to fulfil her true potential both personally and professionally. Orlaith passionately believes that women can be amazing parents and successful businesswomen and shouldn't ever have to compromise on either. When Orlaith's son was two weeks old, she created a community that encouraged women to look at sales and competition differently and to build a community that genuinely supported others.

Within a year of launching, she was personally acknowledged by Facebook and invited to join an exclusive community-building group they host. Orlaith and her son attended 'Facebook gather' where they met Sheryl Sandberg - chief operating officer of Facebook and founder of LeanIn.Org.

Building on her extensive career experience, Orlaith is one of the few business coaches who is both a qualified coach and has a career history in business development. Through combining her two greatest passions (personal development and business growth) she has quickly become a well-known and respected business figure across Edinburgh and beyond.

A firm believer that stories of motherhood can teach us valuable business lessons, she's no stranger to the myriad of challenging situations that parenting ensues and has chosen to capitalise on these, bringing them to the forefront of her work and using them to help women gain deeper understandings around themselves and their businesses.

Running her business as a single mum, Orlaith wants to show people what is really possible when you stop making excuses. She is determined to support other mothers who have decided that they are fed up playing small and want to follow their passions and run their own business.

Website: www.orlaithb.com

Facebook: https://www.facebook.com/TheMumpreneurRevolution/

Instagram: https://www.instagram.com/themumpreneurrevolution/

What Parents Need To Know About Children *What Can Parents & Children Do To Survive Self-Isolation, & Each Other And How To Stay Creative & Keep Your Family Sane During Lockdown*

Lockdown came, and all of a sudden, me and my wife were not just parents to our 4 children (2 boys aged 11 and 8 and a boy and a girl twins ages 2) – we were teachers, exercise coaches, 'pseudo' school friends and chefs.

Being holed up at home with your loved ones can put a strain on relationships, especially when concern about the current circumstances already has sentiments running high.

Ordinarily, there is grandma and grandpa, for extended family caregiving. But with the elderly especially at risk, we found ourselves on our own.

But there are things we can all do to help us get along with our families better, by maintaining strong relationships and avoiding clashes and frustrations during this unprecedented time in our lives.

Establish A Routine

From the onset of Lockdown, the schools were setting the older children work on their platforms. Supervising the learning from home while running the business from home was initially a struggle.

The stay-at-home orders left us stressed without routines, but we quickly found that creating a schedule for our family was a way to regain, even in a small way, a sense of order and regularity.

Whatever your daily routine looks like, the certainty and consistency of this structure can bring comfort to you and your family during these indeterminate times.

We maintain as much 'normal' as we can by establishing daily routines for things like defined morning routines, meal times, exercise times, a specific endpoint to the school day or working day and a calming bedtime.

We have discovered, that it is important to try to delineate week-ends as different. Although this mainly applies to my older children.

During the day we try to eliminate screen distractions as much as possible. However, we appreciate the importance for the older children to connect with their peers and teachers so that they do not feel isolated.

In order to break the day up we create a list one day in advance with 3 different breaks activities that the older children can pick for the following day, and give them 10 minutes to enjoy that break-time activity.

Needless to say, there isn't a one-size-fits-all way to schedule every child. Our eldest son finds security in following a school-like timetable, whereas our middle son thrives on a more child-led, free-flowing approach, but all of our children need some predictability in their lives.

At the end of each day, we set aside time to talk about how our day went, face time extended family members, play a board game, read, or walk the dog.

Limit Exposure To The Media

As the media tries to understand the scope of this unprecedented, global health crisis, its coverage of the coronavirus pandemic has been raucous, to say the least.

And once shared among friends, the quantity of constantly-changing news updates can be disconcerting.

For this reason, I limit myself to only browsing official websites rather than Instagram or Facebook feeds for my daily updates on the pandemic.

We try to keep talking about the Corona Virus to a minimum around the house. Understandably, the older children have lots of questions and we answer them honestly, factually and age-appropriately – but we try not to focus all of our family conversations on the COVID 19.

Embrace Family Time

Being so accessible to each other every day can make it easy to forget to find quality family time and focus on emotional connections.

Against the sad backdrop of the coronavirus, we are rediscovering the pleasure of spending time with each other and our children. Lockdown has been an opportunity to nurture our relationships and enjoy each other's company with fun activities and games such as:

- Zoom – just because the children might not be able to physically be with their grandparents, doesn't mean they can't see them.

- Movie nights – it's the perfect opportunity to bond with all members of the family - and the children cherish curling up with us and each other on the couch and sharing in the experience playing out on the screen. It's the stuff childhood memories are made of.

• Making obstacle courses – as part of our Easter Egg hunt me and my wife created an obstacle course using objects from around the house like boxes, a skipping rope and hula-hoops, and an egg and spoon.

• Board games – from now on Friday nights in the Dattani household will be for games. It's been the perfect way to teach the children about teamwork, patience, and how to win and lose gracefully.

• Jigsaw Puzzles – we've been doing puzzles every day with the twins. Initially, we started with 4-piece puzzles and through lockdown have progressed to 16-piece puzzles. Ultimately, the most important thing is the fun involved in playing with puzzles! The twins enjoy learning the most when they are having fun.

• Reading together – in the evening we have family reading time, where I and my wife read to the twins and the older children get to read a book of their choice. Cuddling up with a storybook at bedtime provides routine and stability, essential for children as they learn best through gentle repetition.

• **Arts And Crafts** - instead of buying bubbles from the shop, we make it into an arts and crafts project. The older children made bubble solution warm water and washing up liquid and made DIY bubble wands using pipe cleaners. The twins and dog spend entire afternoons running around catching them.

• **Gardening** - planting is not only fun but also long-term activity, it's been nice for us to watch the plants the children have planted grow and take part in nurturing and caring for them.

- **Spotting Wildlife** – this has been a favourite with the older children. Since moving to Stanmore in 2016, we'd seen grey squirrels, wood pigeons, magpies, crows and gulls but had never seen hedgehogs, muntjac deer, foxes, green woodpeckers, pied wagtails, red kites, grass snakes, ring neck parakeets, mute swans, robins, Canada geese, Pipistrelle Bats, great tits, wrens, finches, herons, toads an egret and many other species of birds and insects that we haven't yet been able to identify. All within 5 minutes' walk of our house!

- **Picnics and BBQ's** - Whenever the sun is out, we take a blanket and BBQ outside, some healthy foods to make sure we get our daily dose of vitamin D.

- **Housework** – lockdown has been the perfect time to teach the older children to learn what it takes to run a household. We've devised a rota where they each have specific jobs they need to do, like putting away the dishes, hoovering or helping hang up clothes.

Exercise

When compared to the spectre of death and global economic collapse, having to take time off from exercising seems pretty low on the list of calamities caused by the lockdown, but exercise is especially important now, even when the logistics are more challenging because it boosts us physically and mentally.

As well as the physical health benefits, keeping active is a great way to ward off some of the psychological issues associated with being cooped up for an extended time.

I start my mornings with a brisk 30-minute dog walk. He is naturally in the present, so watching him run around helps me think the same, and it puts a smile on my face. It also forces me to go outside, when I might otherwise sit inside on a cold day. When back at home, I do some stretching and breathing exercises.

During the week, we all do a Joe Wicks home workout, although aimed at children the whole family gets involved.

I've found that the simplest way to work out at home is to use your body weight, and for good reason. Push-ups and squats are fundamental pieces of any fitness routine, and you need to hold mastery over them.

They can help you build strength, endurance and burn calories. And by circuit training (going from one exercise to the next, without little or no rest), you keep your heart rate up, burn more calories and get the most out of your exercise time.

Body-weight HIIT workouts are relatively short and don't take up much space. Best of all, they don't require any equipment.

Although as a family we've always eaten relatively healthily, since lockdown we have eaten healthier than we normally would. When in the office I usually buy a meal deal or grab a sandwich for lunch every day.

At home, we put a lot of effort into all of our meals. We always use fresh fruit and veg, season it, take no shortcuts with low-nutrition frozen stuff, and avoid grazing all day on junk food.

Patience And Understanding

At a time when we all face uncertainty and worry about coronavirus, such changes in our relationships are all the harder to cope with. So, it is worth trying to be extra patient and understanding, both with each other and also ourselves.

Being in each other's pockets at all times is bound to aggravate any strain you might be feeling. In the Dattani household, we have designated different areas to different family members and/or uses (e.g. work, play, homework) to ensure we all have space (and privacy) to complete tasks without interruption.

It is also important to encourage time out and space for everyone so they can unwind and have some time alone.

We try to work out a set of boundaries with the children so they understand our expectations and we can grasp theirs too. We build in family time in the day so the children feel supported. Ensuring that they have structure through their day minimises any potential conflict.

The lockdown has meant a different rhythm of life, a chance to be in touch with others in different ways than usual.

To conclude, it helps to try and see this time as a different period in your life, and not necessarily a bad one, even if you didn't choose it.

Our new daily routine prioritises looking after ourselves. As a family, we read more, watch more movies, have a daily exercise routine and have tried new relaxation techniques.

The lockdown has taught us that whenever people are forced to collectively and radically change their daily lives, due to an external event, its brings a shared joint experience that we will continue to talk about in the years to come; a sense of having all been "in it together." We hold onto that feeling. We remind each other that it is in the very near future.

The older children have started keeping a daily diary. It is a great way for them to keep track of quarantine life, record memories and note down aspirations and emotions.

For us, the best thing to have come out of lockdown is that as a family we are letting the outdoors recharge us. As nature heals, so do we. We've been forced to pause, slow down, reflect and appreciate the little things our front and back gardens, local woodland and lake have to offer – from morning birdsongs to the riot of pastel colours pouring from our seasonal blossom trees.

Thanks to quarantine, we have found that there's something beautiful about reconnecting with the great outdoors, whether that's through gardening and nature spotting on outdoor walks.

Ketan Dattani

About The Author

Ketan Dattani is the Founding Owner and CEO of Buckingham Futures, a specialist award-winning Environmental Recruitment Business that provides bespoke permanent and temporary recruitment and consultancy solutions to public and private sector employers.

He has a high profile within the Recruitment sector and is widely recognised as an expert on Employment Law, Employee rights, CV writing and for providing Careers Advice.

Academically he is a graduate of Environmental Biology and a post-graduate of Environmental Planning and Management.

He also holds a Certificate in Employment Law and The Certificate in Recruitment Practice which is a nationally recognised recruitment qualification developed jointly by the REC and key employers.

He began his career in recruitment in 1998 and in 2013 Ketan set up Buckingham Futures.

Business In A Post-COVID-19 World And The Role Of AI In Reinventing Business

In the famous words of Donald Rumsfeld nearly 20 years ago, we are entering a phase of "known unknowns"[1]. That is, we are aware of things we need to know, but we don't know them yet. The world of "known unknowns" is one full of assumptions we cannot validate. In business, we call this a VUCA world – an environment that is characterised as volatile, uncertain, complex and ambiguous. The concept of VUCA has been around since the end of the Cold War in the early nineties. For business leaders who usually evaluate the available information to make decisions, unprecedented events outside the organisation make this process more difficult.

The current COVID-19 situation is a perfect example of a VUCA event that is putting businesses on a crossroad to make a choice. They must choose to either 'batten down the hatches' and try to ride out the storm until the situation improves or continue pushing through these difficult times while adapting to a new world of challenges and opportunities. The problem with the first strategy is that when these businesses re-emerge into the marketplace, both the competition and the customers will have changed and 'business as usual' will no longer exist. For these businesses, the world will have moved on to a new way of operating and they will be left behind. For businesses choosing the second strategy, even today we see great opportunities to re-design their business models, internal processes, supply chains, finances, company structure and people skills. If digital services,

---

[1]Donald Rumsfeld (February 12, 2002). *United States Secretary of Defense.*

emerging technologies and AI were 'nice to have', they are now becoming essential tools for business transformation. Adoption of AI is being accelerated across different industries at a much faster rate than ever anticipated and we are already seeing amazing transformations. Such cases include:

AI In Banking And Insurance

Banking and insurance were two of the first industries to leverage the power of AI algorithms. If you have ever used a price comparison website to get an instant quote for your car or home insurance, be assured that your data was not looked at by a person. If you have ever applied for a credit card online and received an answer within seconds, the decision was most definitely computed by the bank's algorithm based on a set of criteria that determined if you were to be approved. Every time you call your bank and a computer-generated voice prompts you to say in a few words what is your call about, a programme operating on Natural Language Processing techniques is converting your words into a written command which is then understood by the computer and executed seamlessly.

AI In Medicine

In the last few weeks, we have seen the amazing capabilities of AI in medicine on the front page of many newspapers. There have been instances where algorithms have looked at chest x-rays of suspected COVID-19 patients and accurately diagnose the positive cases, in some cases faster than human doctors. In the US, AI models are used to score already confirmed cases with coronavirus and predict which ones are likely to become critical and therefore need intensive care. In Asia, the most widespread use of AI is to track and trace contacts of someone that that has been confirmed to have the virus and thus warn their close contacts to self-isolate.

AI In Retail

For a typical retailer, one of the key success factors is taking the right reordering decisions and that could entail millions of decisions per day. AI integration into the databases containing supply chain transactions can produce insights for the best and most sustainable combination of reordering stock. An example of this is ordering fresh food for supermarkets. AI algorithms can derive probabilities of demand based on geolocation, weather forecasts, demographic profiles, local events and seasonal fluctuation. This data can be then be used to make decisions that produce both profitability and sustainability. Another case of AI is with retailers that use dynamic pricing strategies where the algorithm analyses the relationship between price and demand and moves the price just the right amount. In turn, this means inventory is not left sitting on the shelves for weeks or running out before the next delivery arrives.

AI In HR

Companies that already deploy AI-powered projects in their HR practices report improvement in their data-driven decisions and improvement in employee experience as well as the more widely expected benefits of routine task automation and cost savings. With such powerful AI tools, HR departments can create personalised career strategies for each employee. When employees feel valued and their personal KPIs are aligned with their career aspirations, the company inevitably sees results in improved productivity and engagement from each employee. The second-largest impact of AI is demonstrated in talent acquisition. Many organisations deploy online forms for job applications which are then analysed by an algorithm to shortlist the most suitable and qualified candidates for the position. Given time and data, the algorithm can take this task beyond just automation and learn to 'predict' how well is the candidate likely to fit within the organisation and the level of their productivity.

AI In Marketing

Platforms like Google and Facebook have democratised the use of AI by integrating this technology in their campaign management software. Marketers are no longer required to spend time and money creating complicated customer personas and then trying to adapt their campaigns to best target them. Google can do that for you through smart bidding and sometimes with a higher success rate than the human effort. In the sales stage, AI can also be integrated into the CRM system of the company. Here, methods used by people with best conversion rates can be analysed and patterns extrapolated. A machine learning algorithm can then be trained to handle much larger volumes of enquiries and with a similar rate of success. Email and chatbots have proliferated in the last few years for this same reason.

AI In Manufacturing

One of the early adopters of AI has been companies in the manufacturing industries. The specific strand of AI utilised is RPA – Robotic Process Automation. 2020 has seen a move towards Autonomous Mobile Robots with enhanced flexibility and bigger diversity in application. What this means is that the robot can navigate an unstructured environment. This essentially means they can move around the factory while avoiding bumping into people which is only achieved due to advancements in computer vision. Interestingly, this is the underlying technology behind driverless cars and drone deliveries. As more people shop online due to local lockdown or social-distancing measures, speed of production and delivery will be essential for manufacturers in order to remain competitive. Such high demand cannot be met without some form of automation.

Myths

If some of these use cases have inspired you to consider adopting AI in your own organisation, now is the best time to start your research and preparation so that your business is ready for the post coronavirus world. But before you start, here are a few myths about AI that we need to bust so that your choices are informed by facts.

Myth 1 – My Business Does Not Need To Consider AI

AI technologies have passed the stage where they were considered just a fleeting fashion. The use of AI in larger corporations is so widespread that now in 2020 over 90% of the SME's and larger organisations polled by Gartner have already or are working on an AI strategy for their business.

In a post coronavirus world, many organisations will adopt a cost leadership strategy, i.e. compete by reducing operational costs and thus be able to reduce their prices. Even small businesses will be affected by this move and many will not be able to compete without examining and automating their processes and reducing fixed costs. AI can be one of the tools to achieve this.

Others will look at differentiation strategy where companies make their products or services more personalised to the needs of their customers. Small businesses with a few hundred customers may be able to do this using the existing resources, but even larger organisations are now able to compete on this level using AI. Suddenly, your edge of providing a unique service has been challenged by more and more players on the market.

Myth 2 – AI Can Only Replace Repetitive Jobs

One of the earliest uses of AI technologies was in the area of process automation. Process automation allows people to step away from repetitive tasks utilising programmes with predefined instructions to take over. However, AI has moved on from this basic level and has now evolved beyond improving process speeds to also include process improvements. What we are talking about here is allowing AI to bring about not only automation and speed, but a fundamental change in how to do business, aid the human decision-making process and re-design interactions between people and departments. If business leaders focus purely on automation, they will miss the opportunity to discover methods for improved personalisation and therefore improve the customer experience.

Myth 3 – Once We Implement AI – Its "Job Done!"

Unfortunately, implementing and maintaining AI systems is hard work; this is not a one-off project with a start and finish date. It is true that the beginning of AI implementation is where the work is most intense. For successful integration of AI into the business, leadership must first spend time defining which business issue they are trying to solve. AI may not be the right solution every time and it should not be implemented just because the CEO wants to have it. Here, we need to look at the culture of the company – would employees be resistant to this new initiative because they are afraid that these changes will cost them their jobs or because they don't want to trust and use the new system. Companies then need to evaluate their hardware and software systems and ensure there are budgets available for the implementation of AI. AI is never deployed as a stand-alone programme; rather, it integrates into existing enterprise infrastructure. Data preparation and data cleaning would be the next phase which consumes the most amount of resources and time from a data science, skilled workforce. And finally, the stage that is often forgotten, is the continuous maintenance of the AI system. The business environment continuously changes and that causes AI algorithms to be less accurate overtime as they become less relevant and reliable.

How To Get Started

Implementing AI in your business is hard work, and yet many successful companies are already doing it. In a post coronavirus world, the most innovative, agile and prepared companies will not only survive, but most likely thrive. This will be greatly determined by what these companies did to prepare themselves and how they reinvented their business models while the world was in lockdown and the economies of the world were put to sleep for a few months.

Here are a few practical steps on how to get started on your AI implementation journey:

1. **Increase Your Company's Data Science Competence** – this includes both getting your data ready as well as your people. Spend this time of reduced business activity to fully audit your data – does it need collecting, cleaning or tagging, do you have enough internal data, or do you need to go and look for external data sources. The more 'good' data you have, the

better results the AI models will produce. In the same way people skills can be developed internally or externally to your organisation, you need to consider whether to upskill existing staff, to hire new competencies or to outsource certain aspects to consultants. It may have to be a combination of all three.

2. **Analyse Your Internal Business Processes**–time and effort must be dedicated to understanding in-depth how your business operates its existing processes and workflows. Then it would be a good practice to streamline the tasks so that implementing AI would be effective and efficient from the beginning. Try to reimagine your business without carrying the burdens of past decisions. You should adopt a start-up mindset as if you are starting a new company here and now and think how you would like it to operate in the current environment. This is where AI can link technological solutions with real business value.

3. **Review Your Employees' Jobs** – with the new re-imagined business model, your employees may need upskilling, re-skilling or the business may need entirely new roles. One of the key capabilities identified last year by McKinney's' research of CEOs on skills of the future is digital inquisitiveness defined as: "A habitual inclination to question and evaluate the data before them". Employees that continuously invest time in improving their skills are better equipped to understand the insights provided by AI applications and find ways to implement them in the improvement of the business. Consider investing in an e-learning platform where employees can take courses to understand how AI could be used to improve business processes. These employees will ultimately become the AI champions throughout the organisation and inspire others to also develop the right mindset.

4. **Audit The Company's Existing Technology And Data Systems**— IT is the operational backbone of any organisation. We see it even more today that without the right technology, working from home would not have been possible for many and businesses would have

to close doors permanently instead of just riding the storm out. The technical and AI skills of the people working in the IT department are key to the success of the implementation of AI applications. Historically, the primary driver for IT teams has been to protect it and secure it. Security would remain a top business priority alongside a new paradigm of democratisation of information. What that means, in practice, is to make all relevant information easily available to the right employees to be able to make data-driven decisions.

5. **Develop Realistic Use Cases** - A useful case is a small-scale project where AI is implemented in a narrow area of the business. It is used as a pilot case to answer questions like how the work will be divided between the AI application and the employees. It provides insights on how business processes might need to change, highlights the need for new skills, facilitates the estimation of costs and benefits and, most importantly, demonstrates the business value. When ready to expand AI across the whole organisation, cases that are properly developed can help companies avoid ineffective implementation, waste resources or limit the enthusiasm forAI rollout.

These examples and tips barely scratch the surface of what is possible with the ever-increasing capabilities of AI solutions. In these early days of AI adoption, we are unable to fully calculate the return on investment of such programmes. Where we will see the earliest wins would be in cost reductions and improved efficiency but ultimately where the greatest business value will be seen is when benefits spill over into benefits like improved productivity and enhanced customer experience. Identify the company's bottlenecks and start from there, demonstrating small wins that will be the cases galvanising the rest of the organisation.

Push decision making down the hierarchy of the organisation, where the information is current and solutions most potent.

Taking any step along the AI transformation journey is better than being paralysed by uncertainty and waiting for the world to return to what it was before coronavirus. That is a highly unlikely scenario. All industries are rapidly changing and any organism that doesn't change as fast the environment faces extinction.

Dessy Ohanians

About The Author

Managing Director Certificate and Corporate programmes at LSBF Executive Education, CEO at the London Academy of Trading.

Dessy joined LSBF Executive Education in 2014, to define the strategy and oversee the implementation of that in the area of Professional Development, Executive Education and certificate programmes. In 2018 she also became the CEO of the London Academy of Trading. She has been an entrepreneur for over 20 years, with an extensive experience in the education industry both in the private and public sector.

Dessy is deeply involved in education projects and roles alongside her positions at LSBF and LAT, being a mentor for charitable foundations and serving as governor for two London schools.

In 2017 Dessy also became a finalist in the prestigious Future Leaders Award which has come to be a platform to launch young female entrepreneurs and personalities at the early stage of their career, as well as a confirmation of their achievements and success.

Balancing Children At Home, Maintaining Good Wellbeing For All, Whilst Still Working And Home Schooling

I set up my own business over 2 years ago, and the primary reasons for doing that was to be there for my children. To work around school, ensure I was the one managing the after school emotional fall out, help them to decompress and essentially be present.

I am a conscious business owner, who specialises in working in flow, with energy and enjoy a level of success that enables bills to be paid etc. The best piece of advice I was ever given by my coach was to ensure the energy is balanced - 1/3 on myself, 1/3 on my business and 1/3 on my family.

So, I had got into a groove like so many others, working at certain times of the day, playing at others, and relaxing grown up time once our little darlings had toddled off to bed. When the balance tipped, which inevitably it did, it didn't take too long to get back on track. What it prepared me/us for, is what we are dealing with now. Being in lockdown with our children and keeping business commitments without losing our minds is a very real situation for so many of us.

And when we come out of lockdown, life will not be the same again, thankfully. What I am grateful for is knowing who it is I want to stay connected with, that we do have the opportunity to do nothing some days,

and also know that every day is a learning day whether we are working or schooling.

What we are now dealing with, will have thrown up many emotions and lessons for many of us, not least because we did not choose this situation.

The Biggest And First Lesson Became Surrender

- To surrender to the situation (out of our control)
- To surrender to our humanness (many of us haven't had a chance to ever slow down enough to know ourselves).
- To surrender to something bigger than money and material possessions.

What it has done, and long may it continue, is it has enabled us to strip back to what is most important to us.

Our health, our human connection, our families and love.

Clarifying Routine And Family Rhythm

When this all kicked off, the first thing I did was frantically look up timetables, printable learning aids, get in a bunch of supplies (craft / chalk / paper /paint / glitter) and load up the Ipads with some of the age appropriate apps. I also sought out some of the board games and 'learning through play' toys that would enable us to keep learning when school work became 'annoying'.

I first thought the best approach to get the children through this situation was to attempt to 'school' the children using the timetable the school provided. My girls, though they despised having to get ready for school once there, loved the routine and familiarity.

I realised after one week of trying to replicate that routine, it just wasn't effective, in fact it reinforced to the children how different life was. Here was Mum trying to setup lessons like the teachers but not explaining it in the same way. The end result was two stressed out kids and a stressed out shouty mum. So, my husband and I ditched that approach fairly quickly. We decided that the best approach was to embrace the emotions we were all feeling. So, we encouraged quiet time, imaginative play, scavenger hunts, helping mum with cooking and tidying, and loosely following the timetable we were given by the school.

Finding A Rhythm

Then after a few weeks, we hit Easter break, and we started to introduce the schooling tasks.

This was only after we got a feel for our eldest's natural rhythm, in which she had pockets of time (like all of us) when she was receptive to 'schoolwork'. This for her is early morning, so directly after breakfast between 7 and 9am, and then she has another wave in the afternoon, and sometimes just before bed. So, we have several points in the day when we can tick school work off the list.

We also created physical space in her room where she could sit with one of us to quietly go through her writing and maths tasks, normally the things we do first thing.

Our youngest is different again, she prefers to watch TV or play her imagination games first thing, she'll be ready to engage in play or learning around snack time at about 10ish. As she is a pre-schooler, we still at the stage of learning through play, so it can be more fun and inclusive.

During this time my husband, who is home based, has an 8-hour day to fulfil, thought luckily the company / boss he works for understands there are days he will need to take the kids out for an hour or help out when tempers fray. But essentially, we've have figured out a loose routine whereby I cover schooling in alignment with the kid's rhythms, so it has become a little easier for me to manage my work commitments around them.

I would suggest that this is different for everyone, but it really does make a difference to work with each individual's high and low energy pockets through the day. We have got so used to working 9 – 5; this is not always the healthiest approach for anyone.

We also try to make the day fun. I love heading out for a family walk at lunch time to get the blood pumping, it means me, and husband get some time together, but also the girls can break up the day a bit more.

In short, creating a loose routine which includes time for learning, time to move, regular nourishment, time for rest and time to create - are all important for everyone to thrive mentally and physically. I just hope we can continue once things start to open up.

Managing Emotions

When we moved into lockdowns around the world, this would have set most of us on a roller-coaster of emotions. We won't ever know how it has affected every single person, but I would guess that we are all moving through an element of grief or fear. This is where my point about surrender comes in. There will be grief around letting go of old routines, how we have always done things, 'losing our freedom'. An attachment to things we never really had. We can, all of us, use this time to grow and become totally self-sufficient. To enable us to learn and not to rely on others, for our happiness, and that all emotion is ok.

The best thing we can do at this time, and after COVID-19, is to let the emotions we feel come up safely, acknowledging how and perhaps why we felt that way, and to learn to let them go.

I shudder to think about statics being published around those who are struggling with abuse at this time, I only hope and trust that they realise that being in an abusive situation is not normal and they should reach out for help.

This is an opportunity for us all to really go within and face our demons. Whether that be our addictions, luckily for shoppers Amazon takes a lot longer to deliver; I jest but taking this opportunity to clean up our lives and our habits will never be presented like this again.

Taking time out in our schedules to meditate, journal or just focus on our breath is the ideal way to help process any emotions bubbling to the surface, but also it teaches every member of the family how to be self-sufficient, to breath properly (often the cause for rage / anger / anxious feelings) and process our grief effectively.

When I say let the emotions pass safely, if your child is the one struggling with an emotion, as I have experienced, I found it best to let her rage in her safe space (her bedroom) until she is ready to put a name to how and why she is feeling a specific way. Often when she is unable to express how she is feeling, or is unable to process the emotion, I ask her to draw how she is feeling and describe it to me – it works wonders. If we hold on to the emotion - we cannot move on to the next stage of grief and essentially let it go.

Communicate, Communicate and Communicate

As part of dealing with our emotions, it is essential to communicate those feelings. I ran a little game with both my girls to identify emotions and talk about how each emotion felt. Essentially to encourage them better to explain how they are feeling when something doesn't quite go to plan.

One thing we are finding as a family, is we are dealing with things as they come up more. One habit my husband and I had got into pre-COVID-19, is we would store up all the chat about the children over the week, then have those chats away from little ears in the evening, when we had enough energy.

One thing to help keep energy moving through the home and reinforcing the 'letting go' of difficult emotions, we have now found is to talk about things that bug us as they come up, acknowledge those feelings and move through them.

In the first few weeks, we had many a shouty day, but when we acknowledged it was more frustration and grief around the situation, we were all 'stuck' in, it helped us all to understand that it wasn't personal.

Now I am not saying its ok to hit the roof every time some-one doesn't do something you want them to do, but it still happens especially when we are tired and energetically drained.

One thing to try and break the habit, is if you do find yourself blowing up, is step away, and then to take responsibility for how and why you reacted in a certain way.

Communicating better what it is that has made you cross, goes some way to helping all parties understand how to better handle the situation the next time. If you have kids, they will be watching how you dealt with that situation and it will reflect in your children's behaviour.

What I am saying is it is to OK be human, and to embrace our human emotions. Communicating when we are tired, needing a timeout, communicating when we need help. Parents, splitting the load with kids where possible. Talking about our days and how we are feeling. Writing letters to loved ones we can't see. Organising video calls to check in with our loved ones.

I talk a lot about our family experience, some of us are home schooling - some of us are alone - some of us are with people we are literally getting to know properly - because for the most part most of us haven't spent this long together in a small space for a long time.

Regular meditation will go some way to helping balance all of this.

But, most of all be compassionate with how YOU are feeling. It really is OK.

Tips In Energy Management

We are not designed to sit in each other's spaces 24/7 – some of us sensitive types need space to decompress and clear energy, empaths will need a time out on their own daily to release any energy they may have inadvertently picked up from others. Which is where being balancing being in nature and electronic devices is so important. We may not be able to go out and do new things, but we can mix up how you are approaching your day. Parents, you'll have to work your schedules to manage this, but try to take a day or some time to yourself.

To Just Press Pause.

Step away from all the jobs and the 'must dos'.

It really is ok to stop and smell the roses or catch up on sleep.

If you are practising good self-care, then your children will start to understand it is ok for them to slow down too!

On your daily walk venture to different places, take different routes notice everything - savour it all.

Get creative in the kitchen – enjoy cooking different meals, get the kids involved as part of their learning.

If you are a business owner or have suffered with your job, use this time to brainstorm what you might like to do after the lockdown is lifted. Now is the time to re-evaluate, reset and realign with what inspires you.

The possibilities are endless, now is the time to get your house in order ready for when the doors do open. Take time out to listen to your heart and do what makes it happy.

A Daily Practice

For some of us, there will be feelings of being trapped, not able to go anywhere we please. A claustrophobic feeling. The way to help to change this thought, is to try to reprogram our mind through a regular daily practice. It's our choice how we think and feel.

I recommend that you set an intention that you are going to have a good day. Teach your kids to do it too. It's amazing what you can achieve as a family when you are all pulling energetically in the same direction. And this is something that can continue past COVID-19 and become a regular fixture.

Focus on how you want your day to be.

Ultimately, we have no control over what happens outside, but we can take steps to create a loving space for our family. We need to be fluid and flexible and understand that we can start to build in new healthy habits for all in this our present moment, and for a shiny new future.

Sarah Lloyd

About The Author

Sarah Lloyd – PR Alchemist and intuitive coach – just published her first book Connecting the Dots about being more conscious in our publicity and marketing, and using the media for purpose over profit. Sarah has been in the PR business over 20 years', promoting tech and start-up businesses at a global level – past clients included Emarsys, LG Electronics, Autodesk and Polycom.

She also is a reiki master and weaves her spiritual practices into her day job. She now offers 121 services and guidance to small business owners and authors, who are looking to use PR as a means to promote their business in a way that feels good to them.

She has worked with mumprenuers, female coaches, A Fairy, a Reverend, a Swami as well as building awareness around festivals / wellness events. Sarah is also the host of 'Connecting the Dots' radio show on Wellbeing Radio - where she talks about all things business, spiritual and being a mum!

Never a dull moment, she is also a mum of two and understands the importance of balance – in work, family and in life - after being diagnosed with PND at the peak of career. In order to get well again, she shifted gears, integrated a more intuitive approach to her service offering, and through the support of other business owners in the same situation was able to carve out a business that is successful but also enables her to be present in her own and family's life.

To find out more about Sarah visit: www.indigosoulpr.com

A Frozen Life
Re-Connecting To Motherhood During Lockdown

Before lockdown, life was good. I had reached the point in my life when all three of my children were at school, giving me valuable time alone during the day. My focus was now firmly fixed on building my coaching practice. I was also writing again, taking advantage of long brackets of peace and solitude. I even found time for myself and I was starting to connect with 'my people'. You could say that after fourteen years of having a child at home, I was enjoying getting to know myself again and regaining a part of my life that had long been neglected.

Then Life As I Knew It Stood Still

It stood still for all of us - what I now refer to as, 'The Great Freeze of 2020.'

I am strongly opposed to being forced to do anything against my will at the best of times, but being forced into lockdown, to ration my food and toilet paper and live in close proximity to my husband and children twenty four hours a day, with nowhere to hide or even shower in peace, really didn't sit well with me at all. How dare I be forced to slow down, and dare I say, relax! My newly discovered life came to an abrupt halt and I wasn't happy.

Clearly mothers around the globe felt the same, as they took to social media to collectively share in each other's pain. Frustrations were being vented about children missing out on weekend sport, and not having enough face to face time with their teacher or socialising with their friends.

A host of other responsibilities were dropped into our laps, things we never expected, like learning grammar and division all over again. I didn't care to know how Jimmy was going to share ten lollies amongst five friends. I did, however, want to know if I was ever going to enjoy my sacred yoga and meditation time in serenity ever again. It was like my life was taking two backward steps when I had only just taken a big leap forward.

Surprisingly though, I actually found myself getting frustrated with the frustrations that were circulating and I couldn't quite understand why it was triggering me so much. Little did I know that I was soon to discover the answer in the most unlikely of situations. As I was trying to come to grips with how I was feeling, my frustration slowly turned into an eerie sense of foreboding. I felt like something big was brewing and I knew I wasn't going to necessarily like it but in hindsight it was inevitable.

It was when my daughter took me by the hand one fateful Autumn morning and led me down the hallway that the sense of foreboding turned to panic, this wasn't "Mummy, I'm hungry", or "Mummy, play dollies with me". The time had finally come for me to sit down with my daughter ... and watch ... Frozen II.

We live in a culture where being busy is a badge of honour. I struggle to recall the last time I made a conscious effort to sit with my children and watch a movie from start to finish. I would always find an excuse to get up and do something else, like fold clothes, make a phone call or do 'research' on Facebook. As my eyes rolled back into my head and I winced in pain at the recollection of my daughter breaking out in song to the powerful lyrics of *Let It Go*, I realised there was no escaping the pending torture of singing snowmen and sage trolls as there was no legitimate excuse for not giving her my full attention.

I had become so fixated on proving that motherhood was not my only defining purpose in life, that I had literally put it on hold while I pursued other paths. It dawned on me that the reason I was being triggered by the frustrations of other mothers, is because I was frustrated with myself. While I was busy connecting with me again, I had disconnected from my children. I was in a panic because I completely lost faith in myself as a mother. I had given the power to screens and teachers and the insurmountable buckets of toys to do the job for me and I had forgotten how to just be with my children.

The realisation that hurt me the most was that, as brutally difficult as it was to put 'normality' on hold for a while, I was completely missing the point. I was being handed a golden ticket to the front row seats of my children's lives... and I was complaining about it! I wasn't being forced to do anything other than reconnect with a part of me that had been truly *frozen*... before lockdown. As the music began to herald the start of the movie, so began a healing process that only Disney could provide. Somehow, watching this movie took on a whole different meaning as I sat there finding myself tuning into a whole host of very clever nuances, messages and themes.

If I was going to give only my own advice on how to reconnect with motherhood, I could not have come up with such a profound list of insights. Instead, as I watched Frozen II, I was amazed at the wisdom contained in this children's film, all I had to do was pay attention. Following are nine powerful insights on how to reconnect with motherhood that I discovered amongst villains, trolls, snowmen and heartfelt romance.

'Control What You Can When Things Feel Out Of Control'

I know I'm not alone when I say that all sense of control and perfectionism goes out the window the moment you become a mother. I believe our children are our first teachers in learning to let go of things we can't control. However, there are two very important things you can control as a mother, where you direct your time and your energy. Halting our ability to leave the house to go to work, run our kids around to sporting events and filling our diaries with social engagements has given us the gift of time. We forget that we have always had control over our time but more often than not we choose to give that control to other people. So what if the dishes sit in the sink a few more hours, or the clothes haven't been ironed or no one has a clean pair of underwear. Watch a movie, build a fort, go for a walk or bake a cake. Don't overcomplicate what will make your child happy, your time and positive energy is one of the greatest gifts you can give them.

'All One Can Do Is The Next Right Thing When You Can't See The Future'

All of a sudden, conversations went from "On the weekend can we..." to "When the virus is gone can we..." It can be hard to give a definitive answer or make plans when we don't know what life will be like on the other side of a global pandemic.

However, if we can focus on doing the next right thing, we will see that future faster. Children tend to like routine and certainty and when we can't give that to them their secure little world can suddenly feel unsafe. As parents we can create certainty anchors to help our little peoples' sense of security. Some certainty anchors may include:

A Family Bucket List - This is a great way of setting goals beyond the here and now to work towards. Everyone is free to add things to the bucket that they wanted to do or achieve, and it gives them something to look forward to once restrictions ease.

Secret Girls And Boys Business - This is what we call it in our house but essentially it is a special time dedicated for children to speak privately and frankly about what is going on in their world - their worries, fears, hopes and dreams. When you give a child a safe space to talk it contributes so much to their sense of security and teaches them that the home is a place of trust, openness and honesty.

Identify Family Values - If you are unsure of what the 'next right thing'' to do is, try creating a list of family values. This not only makes all your decision-making easier, but it gives you a moral compass on which to know what the next right thing is for you as a family. This might include *kindness always* or *approach everything with calm* or *everyone has a right to be heard*.

'The Enchanted Forest Is A Place Of Transformation'

We have never spent so much time in our homes as we have during this global pandemic. Instead of feeling like the walls are caving in on you, look for the opportunity to transform your home environment and routines into something different. Aim to make little changes that contribute to your family's creativity, sense of calm and that help strengthen family bonds.

Try Some Of These Ideas:

Encourage Creativity - Help your children build a fort. There is something truly safe about the warmth and dim light of a great fort. Use different furniture to prop up blankets to create multiple rooms and space. Add cushions for comfort, fairy lights for a touch of magic and snacks to keep hunger at bay!

Establish Quiet Time - Quiet time is a screen-free time of peace and reflection. Reading a great novel, browsing the family photo-album or building an amazing Lego model are all great quiet-time activities.

Break Out Of Routine Once In A While - Routine is a family's great friend and saviour. Strong routines make our lives easier and more predictable, but the downside is that they also foster boredom and monotony. Don't get me wrong, I love routines but once in a while it's good to be completely unpredictable. Just look at your children's faces when you serve ice cream for dinner, extend bedtime by an hour or give permission to spend the day in their pyjamas!

'When Nature Speaks - Listen'

Nature has a lot to teach us. Have you ever walked out into your garden and noticed something you never noticed before? A new flower may have blossomed or a plant you never knew you had decided to reveal itself. Nature just does its thing when it's ready and teaches us to relinquish control and just allow life to unfold. Connecting with the outdoors and the rhythms of nature is a wonderful way of reducing stress. I have to admit that my family love their indoor comforts but being in an enclosed space for a long period of time took its toll. The morning sun became our best friend. We encouraged our children to go outside and feel its warmth on their skin as they did a fun activity - kicking a ball, reading, having a picnic. We also took to the local bike track. My daughter finally had the opportunity to learn to ride her bike without training wheels. With looser and more flexible timeframes, my husband found the time to teach her as we all enjoyed the experience of walking, biking and scootering along the bike track and into the nature reserve near our home. Nature teaches us to slow down, and when we slow down, we are able to tune into our internal nature as well. This is the most wonderful way to help your children learn to listen and trust what their bodies are telling them.

'Fear Is What Can't Be Trusted'

The first thing I learnt during lockdown was how intently my children watched my every move. In any unsettling situation they look for my reaction first. They sense fear in my eyes and in my words and I had to learn very quickly to manage my own fear so I could help them manage theirs. Feeling safe is a basic human need but sometimes we can inadvertently disempower our children by being overly cautious instead of seizing an opportunity to empower them by transforming their fear into courage. Teaching them that courage is not the absence of fear, but doing things despite the fear, will be a gift they will carry with them through life. Two powerful ways you can do this is through meditation and affirmations.

Meditation - children are never too young to learn some form of meditation, it's just finding the style that is most suitable to them. In my experience, themed guided meditations work a treat and I find this to be most effective right before bed. The *New Horizon Holistic Centre* has some beautiful meditations for children on Spotify as does the podcast *Bedtime Explorers*. Turn this into a special bedtime ritual you can share with your child.

Affirmations - affirmations are short positive statements your child can repeat like *I am brave* or *I am loved,* and are the quickest and easiest way to rewire an anxious mind. They can help to calm the nervous system and give worried minds something positive to focus on as they drift off to sleep.

'Throw Yourself Into Something New'

Being locked down, you may be restricted with family outings but while you are at home you are only restricted by your own imagination. There could not be a more perfect time to revisit all the things you said you would do with your children when you had time. Establish some new traditions. Instate date night with your child where you bond over a favourite TV show or movie, order some pizza and allow the 'sometimes foods' to be a suitable dinner option. Why not go through all those recipe books collecting dust on the shelf and choose something special to make where your child is head chef? Why not make your sacred yoga time a shared experience? You may find that you share a special interest with your child you would not have discovered had you not slowed down and given some time to trying something new together.

'Show Yourself'

Give your inner child permission to have some fun! Let your crazy, carefree self be seen, regardless of the eye rolls and gagging gestures from your children. Sometimes we allow life to get so serious that we forget how to be human. Why not put a family playlist of music together and show your children how great your dance moves are? Never underestimate the power of your smile to a child. It lets them know that everything is going to be okay. One of the most important ways we can connect with a child is through emotion. It is okay for your child to see you sad just as much as it is important for them to see you happy. The key is to also show them how to work through those emotions positively. It lets them know that it is safe for them to do the same but also models these skills so they can work through their emotions on their own.

'Step Into Your Power - You Are The One You've Been Waiting For'

The moment lockdown was imposed, mothers everywhere began doubting their ability to take care of their own children's needs, rather than seeing it as an opportunity to 'level-up' and reconnect with their innate ability to raise happy children. At times it seems much easier to relinquish control to other means, both human and non-human. We read all the parenting books, listen to all the advice and attend all the mums and bubs classes because we think we aren't doing enough or giving them enough, yet we forgot that being able to know and truly see our child and what they need, is perhaps the most important skill of all. This is a skill we didn't need to learn because we had it all along. You don't need to look outside yourself for all the answers. Every parent is an expert on their own child. Acknowledge all the goodness you bring to your child's life and accept that what you have to give is enough.

'You Are A Gift'

In whatever capacity you show up for your kids - you are a gift. We can be so darn hard on ourselves when we don't measure up to the perceived notion of a perfect mother. Perfectionism is an illusion we get lured into by social media, unsolicited parenting advice and our own inner critic. We then judge ourselves for falling short of our own high expectations and then sever the connection to our children because we think it's too late to ever fix it. The truth is, there is always time and there is no better time than now. At the end of the day, your children only want to know three things - are they loved, are they safe and what's for dinner tomorrow night? You are already your child's hero; you don't need any other validation than that.

I hope more than anything that this global pandemic allows us to realise the infinite possibilities that can arise from being forced to stop and take stock of what is right in front of us. What if this moment in history was a call to defrost? Motherhood is not able to be frozen. It happens whether we are present for it or not. This doesn't mean we put our own life on hold and pander to everyone's demands. As a mother, it is so important that we allow ourselves to grow and evolve or life becomes stagnant and we become resentful of our little people. It's not about freezing our children out to pursue new paths; it's about allowing them to be part of the journey.

Lenore Pearson

About The Author

Lenore is an author, transformational coach, meditator and speaker. Her background in teaching, holistic wellness and meditation allows her to create space for women to get comfortable with being uncomfortable; to dig deep, be vulnerable, get real, fear less and live life authentically.

She also considers herself a Champion of Stress – she's great at it, does a lot of it, but she also knows how to speak its language! With a history of turning the least stressful situations into the most stressful ones, Lenore has grown to understand that knowledge and appreciation of the human body, positive perceptions and living authentically, can take stress from Frenemy to Best Friend Forever.

Her book, Self Ashored, challenges common perceptions people have about life and it offers a navigational tool for moving from healing to growth. When she's not writing, Lenore honestly buys more books than she can read, which is a good problem to have considering how much all this extra learning benefits her clients.

At home in Sydney, Australia, Lenore is 'mum', focussing her love and energy on growing the next generation of calm and kind-hearted humans. She's still working on this.

- Website - www.lenorepearson.com
- Email - lenorepearsonholistic@gmail.com
- Facebook - @artemismhc
- Instagram - lenorepearson_holistic

The Art and Science of Working from Home

I have been a Corporate Flexible Working Implementation Consultant since 2003. This means going into organisations to implement smart, remote, and flexible working policy and strategies, and manage the psychological implications of working from home and online.

Encompassing everything from working with architects, designers, and ergonomic specialists to redesign office spaces, through to scoping and procurement of technology solutions, designing and delivering management and staff briefings, training sessions, and workshops, and offering Executive Coaching to support the mindset to transition to new ways of working.

I say an art and a science because there are several moving parts, and unseen aspects, over and above simply being at home to work. In addition to considering the factors outlined above, there's a checklist of 45 key items I use, some of which I'll discuss here in bite-size chunks.

Boundaries

If, like the vast majority of the world you were thrust into working from home with no time to plan for it, set clear boundaries, both in terms of your working space, and your time.

Working Space

Many are working from their kitchen or dining room table or sofa. When finished working put everything away or to one side and reclaim the space; Clear away the work and reassign it as the dining room table.

Threshold

Even if working on your sofa, once you're done, get up, put your work material away or to one side, and leave the room. As you cross the threshold of the doorway, consider it the same as you would leave the office. When you walk back into the room, you are walking into your living space. Imagine arriving home. Sounds simple, however the psychological effect of not doing so can be devastating, starting with disturbed sleep patterns, and the days all blending into one when multiplied over the several days, weeks, and possibly months you find yourself in lockdown.

Boundaries With Family And Friends

You may also need to set both physical and time boundaries for family and friends, particularly if they are in covid19 lockdown with you. During the times where you are working and on a deadline, make it clear you are not to be disturbed except for emergencies, even if you are just sitting in the den. If you don't cope well with breaking your flow and concentration, also make it clear to friends the times you are not available for a chat or impromptu Facetime or Skype call.

Scope The Work

Strange as this might seem, a key problem I've come up against time and again over the past 17 years is that staff tend to over rather than under work. The problem becomes further exacerbated if the management structure is not sufficiently equipped to manage remote workers; they often then operate with a sense of fear and guilt and seek to 'prove' they are working.

Get clarity on what constitutes a full day's work with the tasks you can do from home. If the average daily output is '5 reports', when those 5 reports are complete, even if completed early, that shouldn't be a cue to do another batch unless the work hasn't been properly quantified and scoped. There is a mathematical reason the work is often completed more quickly from home if you have the right resources, so when you're done, unless you choose to continue, you're done.

Scope The Work–Management Kpis

If you are reading this from a leadership and management perspective, scoping the work is vital in keeping track of what is being done and having a clear warning if staff will not meet targets or objectives. Periodic checking to ensure your team are both OK, and progressing will help keep the business moving if employees are not furloughed and still working.

What's Your Motivation?

If you are not a self-starter or naturally motivated, create deadlines for what you plan to do, and communicate it. If your organisation has an online portal or regular webinar meetings, state what you plan to do. If a structure isn't in place, find yourself an accountability buddy, and tell them what you plan to do by when. It also helps to know your personal motivation strategy for the times where energy and focus are waning yet things still need to be done.

Keep Your Weekends

Unless you already work weekends, those struggling with not having a sense of structure and feel as though the days are all rolling into one, treat your weekends the same as you used to. Go as far as planning activities; it might be movie night, game day, gardening, a home facial, relaxing bath, reading, etc. Choosing activities you're not already doing during the week psychologically gives you something to look forward to, and breaks up the week.

Big Rock Tasks

I got this idea from Brian Tracy and Steven Covey. A great way to avoid procrastination. You decide at the start of the day on your Big Rock Task(s). These are the big or important tasks. This idea is you start the day with your BRTs and slot what I call the smaller 'pebbles' and sand tasks throughout the rest of the day.

Structure

If you are missing a sense of structure, create it. Even when having a lie in, be up at a certain time. Stop for your lunch break. Schedule in a herbal tea, coffee or water break, and a set finish and cut off time. If you have children, build them into the schedule, for example playtime during lunch, or set study or homework time while you do your Big Rock of or Pebble Tasks.

Connect

When I first started implementing flexible and remote working policies within Central and Local Government 17 years ago, the technology we have now did not exist; No iPads, no smart phones, no fibre optic broadband in every home and office space. Skype was around at the start of 2003.

There are so many wonderful ways to connect, so use them. When you're having a break or finished for the day, check in on family and friends. Send a text, WhatsApp, Facebook Message, email, call someone or get screen time. During lockdown and self-isolation, these small but vital human connections can make all the difference, particularly if you're not used to being on your own for long periods of time.

Get Dressed

A great way to set the tone and demarcation for the day is to get dressed. A full suit and tie might go a tad far, however your work skirt, trousers, shirt, and a tie if you prefer anchors you into work mode. From an NLP (Neuro Linguistic Programming) perspective, an anchor is a physical and mental way to access a particular state. At the end of the working day follow your usual routine.

Move

Because the coronavirus working from home commute most likely only involves travelling between your bedroom, bathroom, kitchen, and workspace, it is important to build movement into your day.

For the past 20 years I have been prescribing my Dance Break Sessions for my Executive Coaching clients. Back then you needed to power up your Walkman or CD player, nowadays pull out your phone or head over to YouTube and choose a favourite song.

If you're fit and able to stand up and move; a simple two step is fine. If you suffer from joint problems, a chair dance will do.

If you're able to do it safely use your daily outdoor exercise break to take a walk if running or cycling isn't on the agenda.

Technology Training

I have been designing and delivering online Sessions and Workshops since 2005, and first ran meetings at the British Telecom Video Conferencing Office in London almost 30 years ago, utilising everything from using remotely recorded Teleseminars burnt onto a CD and distrubuted by post, through to various iterations of the latest Video Webinar platforms. If that thought terrifies you, get some training and learn the basics.

We've moved from a world where the progressive few were regularly working online, into a world where every man, woman and their cat and cute dog is running or attending meetings online. At the time of writing I had just logged off from another virtual birthday party.

You can no longer turn to the office technical guru to set things up for you unless you can screen share or hand your screen over, so it may be time to set up and get over any fears around technology.

Online Education and eLearning

Some organisations are no longer providing staff training because they feel staff got enough to cope with, while others would argue that is the reason training is now desperately required. If there are targets in your PDP (Personal Development Plan) or appraisal, this could be the perfect time to brush up on your skills and prepare for when the physical doors re-open.

I run everything from short online Briefing Sessions, Away-Day's and 1-3 Day Workshops, through to online Conferences and Expos, complete with Main Stage, Virtual Breakout Rooms, AI Powered Networking, and Sponsorship Booths, so remain open to what you can do online, rather than focusing on the elements you can't. You may also own what I call "shelf development" gathering dust at home due to lack of time to read or listen to it.

Team Meetings

It is important to connect with team members, either individually or as part of regular virtual team meetings. If you are self-employed start searching for related Groups on LinkedIn, Facebook, and online.

Speak Up

If you are struggling during self-isolation speak up. If your organisation has a HR Department or designated Coach, Counsellor, or First Aider, book yourself an appointment. If those roles aren't fulfilled, speak to a colleague or manager you trust. It is likely that what seems insurmountable for you just requires another perspective or alternative approach.

Change Management

As a Change Management Consultant one of my biggest tasks going into a company is to unfreeze the organisation or team, show the benefits of the change, and get buy-in for the new process or idea. It's not an easy task, because even when change is beneficial and leads to greater efficiency, profitability, or improved ways of working, people still tend to naturally resist.

If you are overly critical as you navigate your way through the coronavirus pandemic, remember we are coping with a complete shake up and threat to our health, finances, way of working, business, social interaction, and overall way of life.

There may be times where the onslaught of bad news, coupled with the restriction of working from home feels overwhelming. Take heart that when you're facing a new system, even something as simple as Facebook or Instagram changing their algorithm or layout, any change to our norm can feel unsettling, so give yourself the time and space to adjust as you move through the cycle.

Push the Boundaries

In old management speak we would call this one thinking outside the box. For me, deciding to work online was a client catalyst. I received a phone call from someone who had read one of my articles in Psychologies Magazine and wanted to book a 1-Day Breakthrough Session. Great. She said she lived in Birmingham. Fantastic, and even better because there is a direct train from Birmingham to Watford Junction and London. She then paused and said: "Birmingham, Alabama."

I then paused. This was way before Coaching and Therapy was done online, and most certainly not an 8-hour Breakthrough Session, so I made a deal. I offered to do the Session by phone; Skype wasn't something everyone had back then, and if I wasn't happy with the outcome or results, I would give her a full refund.

To this day, over a decade later, it is still one of the best Breakthrough and Timeline Therapy Sessions I have ever done. I transitioned from working 99% face-to-face, to the present day which is working 90% online in terms of my Therapy and Coaching Sessions. I started running my in-person 1-3 day Workshops as live, and on-demand Video Webinar Classes in 2016. As one attendee who had experienced, both my in-person and online Workshop put it:

"I thought I would miss being in the room but this has been amazing."

Look at where you can be creative. Work with what you've got. For example, if you are a jewellery designer or have a manual craft, you could offer online tutorials, take us on a tour behind the scenes, or do A Day in the Life of Series.

If you teach a class, take that online. When I received the email a few weeks ago saying they cancelled ballet class; a hobby I took up for the first time at age 47 ½ I immediately emailed back asking if they had considered online classes. Two weeks later I received an email with not just online ballet classes, but tap, jazz, modern and contemporary. Every Thursday at 6.30pm I now align myself in front of the camera and we all get down to our barre exercises.

If you produce food, beverages, or some kind of game, and can safely ship them, how about creating a Lockdown Basket or Goody Bag? If a couple is missing out on celebrating their Wedding Anniversary in style, show the possibility of having Scottish salmon and a bottle of champagne delivered to their doorstep.

Tens of thousands of people at this moment are being driven wild by their kids and most likely running out of ideas. Package up your Top 5 games and offer a bundle. If you developed an amazing educational App, let frazzled parents across the land know.

If you're a make-up artist, women who are used to their regular pampering sessions are crying out for expert guidance on how to tame their eyebrows, touch up their nails, control their hair, and properly moisturise their skin whilst cooped up at home at the mercy of central heating or air conditioning. I could go on for several more pages however I think you get the idea.

Rest

A conversation I've been having a lot with my Executive Coaching clients is about also taking the time to rest, recharge, re-evaluate, or recuperate. Why? Because so many people coming into 2020 were already tired, and I don't just mean physically tired, their mind was also fatigued. If you follow my earlier suggestions around boundaries for those still working, schedule in what I call Self Care time.

What is your idea of rest and relaxation?

What do you enjoy and what brings you a sense of joy?

Who do you enjoy spending time with? Even though we are in lockdown, I will direct you back to my section on Connection.

What fun things which can be done around the house?

When did you last manage several consecutive early nights?

Closing Thoughts

My hope is this whole pandemic is soon a distant memory and we can all either pick up where we left off, or rise from this as though it were a period of reinvention, and get ourselves physically, mentally, and financially back on track with minimum disruption and lag time.

Should it drag on for several months, I hope you find these introductory tips and strategies beneficial. If you would like to book an online Consultation, Executive Coaching Session, Online Team Building Event, or Therapy Session, get in touch.

Marilyn Devonish

About The Author

Marilyn Devonish, The NeuroSuccess™ Coach, has been a Flexible Working Implementation Consultant since 2003, which means going into organisations to implement smart, remote, and flexible working policy and strategies, and manage the psychological implications of working from home and online. She holds a Business Degree, Post Graduate Marketing Diploma with the Chartered Institute of Marketing, and is a Management Consultant, Prince2 Project Manager, and Change Management Specialist.

She is also a Certified Life and Executive Coach, Certified PhotoReading™ Accelerated Leaning Instructor, Certified Trainer of NLP, Keynote Speaker,

Off and Online Workshop Facilitator, Freelance Writer, and Certified Multi-Disciplinary Therapist including Soul Plan Reader, Future Life Progression, Certified Trainer of Timeline Therapy, and Practitioner of EFT, DNA Theta Healing, EmoTrance, Energetic NLP, Access Consciousness, Tarot, Reiki, Archetypal Profiling, Soul Plan Core Issue Therapy, and Hawaiian Huna, having studied out in Hawaii with those from the original lineage. A Personal Trainer for Your Brain, Marilyn blends aspects of neuroscience with personal development to make accelerated performance and mindset changes more easily accessible to all, in a minimum amount of time. She has been a Coach and Therapist since October 2000.

Marilyn is also the Founder of TranceFormations™, a Coaching, Training and Consultancy organisation committed to creating impactful and lasting rapid transformation and change. Her journey into these disciplines started with being diagnosed with what they thought to be early onset Alzheimer's in her 20s and contemplating suicide in her 30s. Having found a quick, easy, and lasting way to turn that diagnosis and things around 20 years ago, she has been working with both individuals and organisations since then to help accelerate their potential and performance.

Website: https://www.tranceformationstm.com
Email: marilyn@tranceformationstm.com
Blog: https://marilyndevonish.com
Free 20-Minute Consultation: https://bookme.name/marilyndevonish
Flexible Working: https://flexibleworking.brizy.site/

Life is an Adventure!
A Journey from the Darkness to the Light

You deserve to be happy, you know that right? It is your birth right to be thriving in a life and a world that brings joy and love into your life. But I know, all too well just how hard life can get. Whether it's a worldwide pandemic as we have all been experiencing, or when life in general gets tough, and you feel like you are barely surviving, sometimes it can be hard to pull yourself out. It can be difficult to see the brighter side of life and it can be difficult to even know where to get help.

In this chapter, I hope to share with you some practical tips that I personally use with myself and my clients. I hope that they offer you ways to move from barely surviving to really thriving in life. To help you transition from the darkness you may feel now and help you to see the light and joy you deserve. *Let's begin.*

What Choice Will You Make?

The first thing you need to do is to make the choice that you want to change your life. This could mean physical changes or it could mean changes in your thinking. Take a moment to ask yourself these questions and answer them honestly:

Do you want to change? Do you really want to change? Are you willing to do what is needed to help you move into a happy, thriving life?

I hope you have answered YES to these questions, because without some sort of commitment, your circumstances won't change.

I remember when I was suffering from depression. Life was hard. I was barely surviving... crashing into bed each night, trying to fall asleep and then trying to fall back asleep when I woke up in the middle of the night. Waking up in the morning, to the alarm. Getting ready for work and then heading out the door. Working hard in a job I no longer liked and coming home to two precious little children who just wanted their mummy, only to feel like I wanted to curl up in the corner and hide away from the world. I was barely surviving and I definitely wasn't living life.

But in December 2012 something happened that made me want to change. It made me want to take action in my life. I basically answered YES to the questions above and I can tell you that was the best decision I ever made. So to begin with, all I am asking you here is to make a decision to take action. By saying yes, it means that you are willing to take one small step on the journey to being happy and thriving in life.

For those of you that may be struggling to say yes, ask yourself why? What is it, in your current "barely surviving" life are you concerned will change? Is this something you are willing to change so that you can thrive?

An Exercise:

Let's go on a journey together. Give yourself 5-10 minutes to really experience this journey. Put some music on, close the door and turn off your phone.

Imagine a little person, a child. And see that child with eyes wide open and full of wonder. This child has the world at their feet. This child can do or be anyone they wish. This child is excited at the prospect of what life will bring to them. This child can't wait to grow up and see their wishes come true.

Now imagine this child is you. Full of wonder, excitement, and happiness. Eager for what the future will bring. Feel yourself connect with this beautiful child. Feel these feelings and emotions radiate through your body. Spend as long as you wish in this feeling.

So, with that said can you please say, "YES" really loudly to make the commitment to yourself that you want to make changes and you are willing to take action now. Let's continue…

Exploring Life Outside The Box

We all live in a box. Yes, you live in a *box* that is your "norm". It's your comfort zone that has evolved since the moment you were born until today. Your parents and family inadvertently began putting you in a *box* when they gave you "boy" toys or "girl" toys. When they told you what was good and what was bad. When, they told you what to wear and what to say. Quite often this has been done out of love. They wanted to keep you safe and they taught you what they knew.

Then you went to school and your teachers told you how to sit in class and how to answer questions. Your friends and peers told you how to act and how not to act.

And then when you grew up, society also told you what you can and can't do. The society you grew up in has had a huge influence on the *box* you live in. They may have told you to get a trade, or to go to university. They may have told you who your friends should be or who you should marry. All of these factors influence this *box* you live in. I'm guessing you may not even realise you are living in a *box*. The parameters or rules you have placed on your life. The things you will and won't do. The way you believe life should be led.

So Now Let's Ask Some More Questions:

Is there life outside my *box*, or comfort zone?

What do I believe? (e.g. what you can and can't do in life)

What do others believe?

Why do I believe what I believe? (i.e. how have others influenced you?)

How has this helped me in life?

How has this held me back in life?

This *box*, quite often not only keeps you living within the confines of fear (so you don't step outside of it), it also influences your beliefs. Your beliefs have been shaped over many years of conditioning. Things you have been told, things you have experienced, and things you just choose to believe because it's easier then changing your beliefs. All these beliefs shape who you are, who you choose to believe and whether or not you can move through any fears.

What you believe will occur in your life, will quite often occur because that is where your attention is. That is what your expectation is. So that is what you will see play out. Your life will play out just as your parent's life has played out or how the society you live in expects your life to play out.

Let Me Share A Story To Illustrate.

I was the eldest of 3 children born to parents that had immigrated to Australia. I was the eldest with two younger brothers. Both my parents worked very hard to provide for us. They saw Australia as the land of opportunity and knew if they worked hard, then they would be paid well and be able to provide for us.

When it came time for me to finish high school I was expected to go to university. My father was never given the chance to go, even though he was definitely smart enough. But being the youngest in his family, back in Yugoslavia (now Croatia) it just wasn't possible.

As I was quite intelligent myself, he wanted me to go to university because he never had the chance. His belief was going to university would mean better career opportunities and I thought I believed the same thing. I still remember going in and choosing my subjects. I really didn't know what I wanted to do but I was the good girl and didn't know any better. My family and the society I lived in, expected me to go to university and get a degree.

But something didn't feel right. I didn't know what it was but I didn't want to go to university… at that time. I didn't know how to tell my father. Fortunately I had just started dating my boyfriend who was extremely supportive. He helped me find the courage to tell my father that I wanted to defer going to university. Both my parents were surprised at my decision but supportive. They just wanted me to be happy. When you make a decision in life, there are times you will be supported. There are other times you will not be supported. The important thing to do here is to find people that will support you in any decision you make. Find people that already live outside your *box*. These are the people that will help you or inspire you to make the changes you need to make.

An Exercise:

Other people's life
Other people's life beliefs
Other people's life actions

My life
My beliefs
My actions

Spend five to ten minutes contemplating the box you live in. Draw a box and inside of it write down everything that is part of your life. Every person, every belief, every action. Then on the outside of the box write down the people, beliefs and actions that sit there. Take note of the things you wish were inside of your box.

Overcome Fear

So let's ask a few more questions:

What changes do you want to make?

Do you believe you can make these changes?

Do you have people in your life that will support you?

After asking these questions do you feel fear creeping in? You may hear yourself say:

Don't ask such questions. It's not safe to leave the comfort of and confines of my life.

What will my parents, siblings, friends say?

What will my partner say?

And if you listen to these inner voices, then any fear you have will grow.

Fear can be crippling. It can stop you from really living life, but even more damaging it can prevent you from making the changes you need to make.

So, what is fear? Essentially fear is an emotion that arises from a perceived danger. And that danger can be real or imagined. It can be physical or emotional. Either way, it's important to remember that fear is an emotion. And any emotion is really nothing more than a feeling at a point in time in your life and as with all feelings, it will move on. Chances are you are feeling something right now as you read this chapter, and you felt something different last night or this morning. Consider how you feel when you see a loved one? What about someone that you feel intimated by? All these emotions are just a feeling at a point in time and they do change.

So how do we overcome fear? Firstly you need to be honest about exactly what you are afraid of.

Are you afraid of what people will say?

Are you afraid of leaving your house?

Are you afraid of getting sick?

Are you afraid of not having enough money?

Being comfortable in a situation, even when it's not bringing you joy can sometimes seem easier than making changes and taking action.

Let me share another story. Prior to 2012 I was suffering from depression. I had been for many years. This was despite my "outside" world looking fine to everyone around me. I had a great husband, two beautiful children, and I was successful in my career. What could be wrong? I would ask myself this constantly, "How can I be unhappy when everything is going well for me?" That question only served to deepen my depression. I couldn't logically figure out why I was depressed.

I finally choose one December day in 2012 to finally get help. The help I chose was a spiritual counsellor. I wanted to know WHY I was depressed. I didn't want to mask it. From the start of our sessions it became apparent that I was living my life for everyone else. I was scared of making changes as I thought that if I did, I would lose the love of those around me. The fear of loss kept me living a life I had begun to hate. Once I had that realisation, I started to work through the fear and realised that the fear of staying the same and continuing to live my life without change was so much greater than the fear I had of making changes.

An Exercise:

Let's answer some more questions:

How will I feel in ten year's time if my life is exactly as it is now?

What will my life look like if I make the changes I want? (you may not know what those changes are yet, it may just be a feeling)?

What changes am I willing to make? (even something small)

Do I think I will lose my partner, my family, my friends if I change?

Am I **more** afraid of staying in my *box* or am I **more** afraid of making a change? What would I regret more?

You can't know anything for certain. Stepping outside of the *box* you have lived in all your life may not be easy, but it is worth it.

Life Is An Adventure!

Yes, life *is* an adventure. Life is not meant to be mundane, boring, tedious or repetitious. Sure, there may be moments in life that feel like that, but life is meant to be LIVED!

One of the first things I realised when I was healing my depression was that I was running away from life. I was doing what was expected of me or at least what I thought was expected of me. I had a well-paid job as an Office Manager for an international manufacturing company. I was married with two healthy children. I was paying off a mortgage in a good suburb. I was living what I thought was a "normal" life. Except this life was literally killing me... my feelings of depression was leading me into a dark hole.

I was running away from really living life because for me it was scary to do anything I thought was not normal. I loved to read. I loved to learn. And I was super passionate about natural healing and all things spiritual. But up until that point it was just a hobby. I couldn't make a living out of it. I had actually had an ex friend tell me so and that belief stayed with me until I chose to change things. I chose to see life as an adventure.

I started to ask myself questions like, "Will I regret doing this or not doing this?" That question became the most powerful question I would ever ask (and continue to ask). This led me to start my kinesiology business, part time at first and then a few years later full time. This question also encouraged me to write my first book, Empowered Happiness – Discovering Bliss Beyond Depression. This question made me say "yes" to a corporate speaking engagement in front of over 130 people (mostly men). This question has helped me really live my life and see that this wonderful thing we call living is really one big adventure. Some things turn out well and others not so well... but it's the adventure that brings joy (and sometimes tears) and real life living!

So let me say it again... **LIFE IS AN ADVENTURE**. How are you currently living your life? Are you barely surviving in a mundane experience listening to everyone around you on how you should live your life? Do you want to start really living life and really thriving in life?

An Exercise:

Imagine a life where money was no object. Where you are really happy. Where you are truly thriving. If you are struggling with this, draw inspiration from television shows or movies you may have watched. There may be a character that you love or a wonderful life you have seen in fiction. Imagine yourself living that life. Where do you live? How do you wake up in the morning? What do you eat? How do you look? Where do you work? Who is around you?

Imagine Living This Life For One Full Day.

At the end of this day, ask yourself, "How do I feel?" Really immerse yourself in the feeling.

Spend time writing down what came through for you. And remember the feeling you had at the end of this day. It's the feeling that is the key to helping you overcome fear and exploring outside of your box.

Brain Frog... Oops I Mean Brain Fog

So now that you are ready to explore the adventures that await you outside of your box, you may feel a little, or maybe a lot, of stress creep into your life.

Stress is a state of mental or emotional strain or tension stemming from an unpleasant or demanding circumstance. These circumstances can be physical or emotional, real or imagined. The interesting thing about stress is that our brain can't really distinguish between real and imaginary. So if you are stressed about a past event or anxious about making changes for your future, your body responds the same way and goes into action releasing stress hormones ready for you to fight or flee.

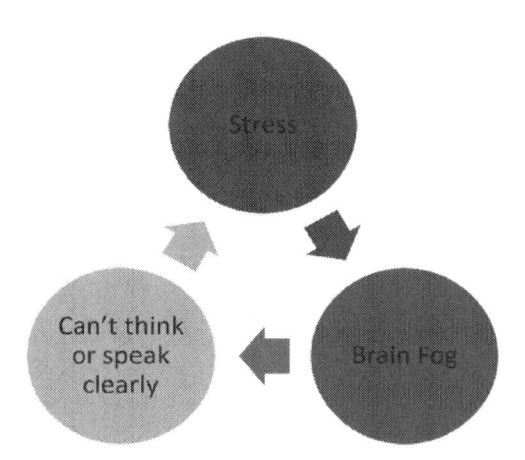

Stress → Brain Fog → Can't think or speak clearly → Stress

The problem with this is that once these stress hormones are released, they flood your brain impacting the way you think and process information. This can then cause confusion on how you should move forward and creates a condition I like to call Brain Frog... oops, I mean Brain Fog. This condition then clouds your thinking, you get more stressed and frustrated and then it increases the Brain Fog, creating a perpetual cycle of increasing stress.

While a little stress can be good as it helps to motivate you to move forward in life, too much stress has many detrimental effects on your body, including

- Increasing your heart rate and increasing activity in the amygdala or fear centre of your brain.
- It can possibly shrink your brain as you lose synaptic connections between the neurons. This then impacts your prefrontal cortex that regulates concentration, decision making, judgement and social interactions.
- Makes learning harder as it becomes difficult to take in and process information.
- Affects memory.
- Affects digestion, muscle tension, your ability to sleep soundly and the list goes on.

An Exercise:

While it may be impossible to eliminate stress entirely, here are some of my favourite things to help reduce stress.

Meditation

Meditation helps to reduce mental chatter and bring awareness back to your breath. There are many different types of meditations that can help you relax, including guided, music, repeating a mantra, breathing and relaxing your body. Insight Timer is a great app that has many fantastic meditations you can listen to for free.

Mindful Emotional Stress Release

An exercise I share with my clients is to place your hand over your forehead and breathe deeply, in through your nose and out through your mouth.

Bring your attention to the room you are in, engaging all your senses – sight, smell, sound, touch, and taste.

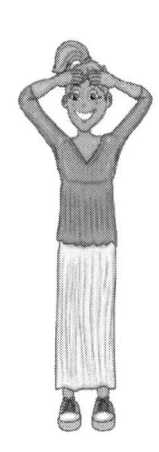

What can you see?

What can you smell?

What can you hear?

What does your forehead feel like under your hands?

What can you taste in your mouth?

By placing your hand on your forehead, you are encouraging blood flow to the frontal cortex of the brain and regulating the amygdala's fight, flight or freeze hyperarousal response.

By consciously bringing your awareness to your breathing you will help increase your oxygen levels, which is needed by your entire body.

Connecting To Your Heart

Now that you have reduced the stress that creating change may have brought into your body, reconnecting with your heart is the next step. mBIT and many other modalities actually acknowledge the heart as another brain. According to www.mbraining.com

> The heart's neural network meets all the criteria specified for a brain including several types of neurons, motor neurons, sensory neurons, interneurons, neurotransmitters, proteins and support cells. Its complex and elaborate neural circuitry allows the heart brain to function independently of the head brain and it can learn, remember, feel and sense.

From my clinic experience I have found that many people tend to lead their lives and make their decisions from the head thinking, when you learn how to connect with your heart magic happens, you will begin to live your life from your truest desires.

Remember I said at the start, YOU DESERVE TO BE HAPPY!

Say that with me…

I Deserve To Be Happy And Successful And Thriving In Life

Your Heart Brain is actually the one brain that can help you truly feel what happiness looks like for you. And it's the feelings that are important. Your head brain is great for logic and helping you plan how you want to make changes. It knows left and right, black and white, logic and creativity, but your heart brain is not polarised by opposites. It feels and truly understands your deepest desires. By connecting to your heart brain and then making decisions guided by your heart, while also integrating your other brains, you begin to experience a life that is meant for you.

An Exercise

Give yourself five to ten minutes of quiet time.

Start by deeply breathing in and out. Allow your body to relax. As you feel more relaxed start to imagine that you are breathing into your heart and out of your heart. Imagine your breath energising your heart. As you do this you, remember a feeling from the past that brought you joy. Allow this joy to fill your heart. Feel this joy start to expand beyond your heart and into your entire body. Sit in this space for as long as you wish. This loving, joyful feeling is healing for your entire mind, body and spirit.

Appreciating Gratitude

It is so easy to find the things in life that are annoying. The person that cuts you off in traffic, the angry shop assistant or the continual bad news you may see on the television. The problem with this is the more you see it, the more you think about it. And the more you think about it, the more you see it.

Gratitude is a powerful way to shift your energy and your awareness of the world. By training yourself to be more grateful of what you do have, you start to make physical changes to your brain and how it perceives the world.

The UCLA's Mindfulness Awareness Research Center has recently shown through their research that:

> Having an attitude of gratitude changes the molecular structure of the brain, keeps grey matter functioning, and makes us healthier and happier. When you feel happiness, the central nervous system is affected. You are more peaceful, less reactive and less resistant.

How cool is that? By being more grateful in life and increasing your happiness, you are actually changing the molecular structure of your brain which in turns helps you to be healthier and more peaceful. I just love that, don't you?

The fantastic people at the Institute of HeartMath have also been doing brilliant work on how the heart beats out a different message when you feel positive emotions like gratitude, love or appreciation.

```
        Feeling
       Gratitude
      ↗         ↘
Life                Happiness
becomes    ←        Increases
more
beautiful
```

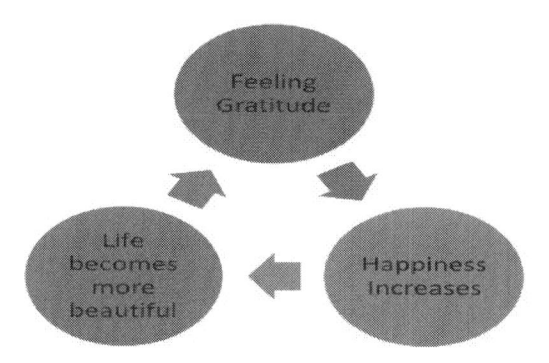

These different messages then determine what kind of signals are sent to the brain. When you train yourself to become more grateful of what you have, life becomes more beautiful and it's easier to see more things to be grateful for. It is a perpetuating positive cycle that only increases with time.

One way we can become more grateful of whatever have in our lives is to become amazed at the little things and to be curious of everything. See things as if you are seeing them for the first time.

An exercise

Imagine you are a small child entering the room you are sitting in for the first time. What are you seeing? Is there something that catches your curiosity? If so, pick it up and explore it. It could be seeing how a stapler staples paper, or how a pen writes on a piece of paper. Look at the colour of the ink or the indentation on the paper. Spent some time really exploring, the wonderful things around you.

Another exercise is to write down 3 things you are grateful for every night. Try to make them different each night. It could be the roof over your head, your warm bed, your full belly or anything else that comes to mind. The more things you find to be grateful for, the more things you will realise you have to be grateful for.

Mindfully Mindful

A powerful way to increase the gratitude in your life is to learn to become more mindful. Mindfulness is essentially placing your awareness on the present moment, while calmly acknowledging and accepting your feelings, thoughts, and how your body feels.

Sadly, in today's society, many have forgotten what it's like to slow down and really appreciate their surroundings, without judgement. Have you? Do you fly from one task to another, ticking off your to-do list and missing all the beauty that surrounds you?

For example, have you ever driven your car somewhere and arrived at your destination only to realise you remember nothing about your journey? Or started eating a packet of chips and then suddenly noticed all you had left in your hands was an empty packet? These are some common examples of 'mindlessness' – a state often referred to as being on autopilot. On autopilot you tend to get lost in doing things so you find yourself constantly striving and struggling to get stuff done instead of really living.

Being mindful starts with accepting yourself, your life and where you are right now. There are many benefits to bringing mindfulness into your life but the single most important one is that mindfulness will influence the levels of happiness in your life. Learning to become more mindful is really not that difficult but it may be something that you do need to learn as many of us weren't taught this when we were growing up.

Here Are My ABC's Of Mindfulness That Anyone Can Follow:

Appreciate - Each present moment, whatever you are doing. Gratitude positively impacts your heart and increases awareness of the present moment. Stop right now and just appreciate that you have this book in your hand and you have eyes that allow you to read it.

Be Still - We're human beings, not human doings. Practice being at peace within yourself each day. Notice how your body feels right now while breathing deeply.

Clean House - Remove the negative thought patterns from your mind by catching yourself as you become aware of them. Also remove any people or responsibilities that aren't serving you. If you can't fully remove them, then reduce the amount of time you spend with these people or responsibilities.

An Exercise

It all starts with you having **YOU Time**, 5 minutes every day. Just stop and observe the moment.

Engage all your senses –

See what is around you?

Feel how your body feels?

Smell the fragrances in the air.

Listen to the sounds.

Taste and enjoy what you are consuming.

Start to bring this into your daily tasks. Engage your senses while you are going about doing your chores, like washing the dishes, or eating lunch. These are called Micro Mindful Meditations and can be included in your life at any time.

Don't Forget To Play

When you were a teenager, you probably wanted to be seen older than you were. And then, when you hit your twenties, you were suddenly thrust into the adult world where you were expected to act "mature" and fit into what society expected of grownups. Sure, physically your body matured with age but that didn't mean you couldn't have fun and play. Many seem to have forgotten the importance of joyful play or even how to play.

You put away your toys, your books, your games. Adult responsibilities take over and time is filled with "to do" lists and "busyness". There's just no time to play. And with everything else taking priority, playing is not important... it's a waste of time! And even if you do find the time to play, feelings of being judged by others as being immature, goofy, or just silly infiltrate your mind.

The sadness in this, is that play is important at any age. Repeating the same chores each and every day, whether at work, maintaining your home or caring for your family increases stress and reduces overall happiness in life. It is ironic that at a point in your life when you need to play the most, you play the least.

Playing Has So Many Benefits Including:

- It promotes more smiling and laughter which leads to more joy
- It helps you to relax
- It increases your creativity and imagination
- It recharges you
- It increases your energy
- It is emotionally balancing
- It can trigger the secretion of BDNF (Brain-derived neurotrophic factor). This is a substance necessary for brain cell growth.
- It stimulates growth in the cerebral cortex
- It improves memory
- It releases endorphins which trigger positive feelings in the body. This can help relieve stress and depression. Endorphins are also a natural pain reliever
- Playing while exercising can make exercising more fun
- It helps you to become more productive in your jobs and in your life; and
- It improves your overall wellbeing.

Do You Remember How To Play? Try To Remember Back To When You Were A Child.

- What did you like to do?
- Did you like to play with others?
- Did you like to play on your own?
- What type of play did you enjoy?

Here Are Just A Few Examples To Help Get You Started:

- Run around under a sprinkler
- Blow bubbles
- Colour in
- Draw
- Play a silly game of soccer
- Play a board game
- Paint, or even better, finger paint
- Write a story using your imagination
- Play with Lego or Mecano

Or My Personal Favourites Are

- **Play The Thank You Game** – Say thank you every time someone does something nice for you. Keep track and notice how many times you can say Thank You in one day. See if you can beat your score.
- **Play The Smile Game** – How many people can you smile at today? Keep track and see if you can beat your score. It's a lot harder to be depressed when your body is showing the signs of joy and happiness.

- **The Meditation Game** – Allow yourself to go on a journey to wherever you mind wants to take you. It could be back to your childhood, to another country or even another planet. There are no restrictions on where your imagination can take you.

And then when you have spent some time in play, notice how much more vibrant and youthful you feel. You will also notice that you are genuinely smiling more, and joy will naturally radiate out.

An Exercise

When you have more time to play in life you know you are thriving in life. Find ways today to play more and have some fun. Make a list of things you love to do and then make the time to do them.

*****

Thank you for reading my chapter. I hope it has offered you the tools you needed to journey from darkness to light. Please reach out if there is anything I can help you with and remember that *Happiness Starts with a Smile and Empowerment Starts with a Choice!*

Carolyn King

About The Author

Carolyn King is the owner and founder of Empowered Happiness and has helped thousands release negative emotions and trauma assisting them to transition to a more fulfilled and happy life. She uses a multi-disciplinary approach which includes kinesiology, mBit and Mindfulness coaching, tapping, NLP, Reiki, creativity, oracle cards and meditation. She is a Kinesiologist, mBit / Life / Mindfulness / Happiness Coach, Reiki Master, Master Lightworker Practitioner, Meditation Facilitator and Angel Intuitive. She is also a corporate speaker, blogger, and international author of *Empowered Happiness, Discovering Bliss Beyond Depression* and has co-authored many other books.

Carolyn King is on a mission to help people live a fulfilled life with real and lasting happiness and is especially passionate about helping those that have hit their rock bottom as she has personally overcome the lows and disconnectedness of depression and the anxieties and stresses associated with corporate burn out. She has studied many different healing modalities and continues to develop her skills, integrating them into her life and creating programs for her clients with the intention of empowering more people.

As a special gift to every reader Carolyn is offering a free download of her, **Pink Heart Activation Meditation**, to help you reconnect with your heart. Head on over to http://eepurl.com/dG-sHH

You can reach Carolyn at the following:

Website: www.empoweredhappiness.com
Facebook: www.facebook.com/empowerkin
Facebookgroup:
www.facebook.com/groups/creatingempoweredhappiness
Instagram: www.instagram.com/empowered_happiness
Linked in: https://www.linkedin.com/in/carolynking-1/
YouTube:
https://www.youtube.com/channel/UCpm6WsN5Pz0y1t8DRdS8XWQ
Email: Carolyn@empoweredhappiness.com
Insight Timer: https://insighttimer.com/carolynking

Foods To Boost The Immune System

Love Your Immune System

Are you curious to find out how changing what you eat might help your immune system? Up until now, you probably haven't given your immune system much thought – yet it's been quietly keeping you safe since you were born!

Your immune system is your best friend. During the Corona-virus pandemic, more than ever, you need your best friend, to keep you safe. Best friends - are friends for life – quite literally!

Just like any friendship, you need to treat each other with respect. Treat your immune system with love and kindness, and it will reward you by warding off horrible infections, cancer and heart disease too. Mistreat your immune system and it will let you down, sometimes with serious consequences.

- What's the best way to look after your immune system?
- How is your immune response affected by what you eat?
- What are the best foods you can eat to support your immune system?

I sincerely hope you will understand that this chapter is not just a long list of healthy foods. To improve your immune system, you need to eat to live – not live to eat. If you can understand the connection between what you put in your mouth, and how this affects all aspects of your health including your immune system, this will help motivate you to make major positive dietary changes for the long term.

Only 5% of Americans are estimated to currently be at their correct weight due to a healthy combination of eating the right foods and taking the right amount of physical exercise. That's a staggering thought! So, this chapter is for the 95% of you who really need to make some serious changes.

So ... let's get started.

What Is The Immune System?

Let's begin with a brief, overview of the immune system. We can only marvel at the infinite numbers of complex, inter-related, and sophisticated, biochemical reactions taking place in our bodies - a gigantic, microbiological fairground - making us what we are today.

The Immune System

The immune system is a highly complex network of specialised white blood cells - lymphocytes, neutrophils, monocytes, and macrophages - which are constantly circulating in your bloodstream. These cells travel inside lymphatic channels, which run alongside your blood vessels. Lymphocytes are stored at various sites in your body, for example, in your lymph nodes, and also in your spleen. They are called to action when a defence is required.

Function Of The Immune System

Your body is constantly under attack from the outside world. Any cell it does not recognise as one of your own is a potential threat and needs to be destroyed. These foreign invaders include bacteria, viruses, protozoa and fungi. However, any of your own cells which have been damaged, and are not fit for purpose, are also killed and removed in the same way. These cells may be early cancer cells. Your body is working tirelessly, 24/7, to protect you and keep you well.

T Cells And B Cells

There are three types of lymphocytes – T lymphocytes, B lymphocytes and Natural Killer (NK) Cells. They pass messages to each other via the release of specific molecules which act as chemical messengers. The immune response involves highly sophisticated, cell-signaling pathways.

T Lymphocytes – known as T cells, are involved in cell-mediated immunity. This is an immune response which does not involve antibodies. Once a cell is identified as foreign, special proteins called cytokines, are released. Important cytokines include interleukins, interferons and tumour necrosis factor (TNF-alpha). The release of cytokines signals the arrival of macrophages, cells which physically - 'eat up!' - the foreign cell - and destroy it.

B- Lymphocytes – known as B-cells, are involved in producing an antibody response. All cells carry shapes on their surface called antigens. Your body learns which are yours and which are not and remembers this. As soon as your body recognises a foreign antigen, it produces an antibody, which sticks to the foreign antigen, and neutralises the attack. Anti-bodies are immunoglobulins, special proteins - made-to-measure for the job.

When The Immune Response Is Switched On – This Causes Inflammation:

Acute Inflammation – this occurs, for example, when a streptococcal bacterium settles on your tonsil. The tonsils are red, swollen, and painful and you have a fever.

Chronic Inflammation occurs, for example, when you develop an on-going problem such as osteoarthritis in your knee. The knee continues to be red, hot, swollen and painful. Chronic inflammation, however, has negative health consequences for your body. Read more about this further on.

What Does The Immune System Need To Function?

For your immune system to function correctly, all the components need to be fully functioning and in good working order. These biochemical processes require essential macronutrients e.g. fats, proteins, carbohydrates, and micronutrients e.g. vitamins and minerals.

Your body is just one great big machine. Like a car which needs petrol, oil and new spark plugs, your body needs the correct food, water, and nourishment. How do we know this? Let's look at this from the opposite angle - malnutrition greatly increases your susceptibility to disease.

Malnutrition Doesn't Only Affect Third World Countries – It Also Affects The Western World

Malnutrition is a major recognised cause of immunodeficiency. Sadly, in third world countries, extreme lack of food results in weight loss. There is a general break-down of gut-barrier function, making it easier for pathogens to pass through the gut wall into the body. Weakness, loss of appetite and dehydration further compound the problem. Overall, this results in a weakened immune system. More than half of children under age 5 die because of increased susceptibility to infections such as measles, malaria and HIV.

However, the problem is not unique to the third world. Even in civilised countries, much of the population is undernourished. In the USA, 15% of the ambulant populations are malnourished, as are 25-60% of patients in long term care and 35-65% of those in hospital.

In the USA, 37 million adults are hungry, including 11 million children, according to the website Feeding America.

Even those who are eating, are living on fast and processed foods, and many have no idea of the dangers. In his fascinating 2018 paper in the *Journal of Lifestyle Medicine*, Dr Joel Fuhrman describes the dietary habits of Americans as 'fast-food genocide.' 71% of Americans are now obese – that's 100 million people.

Today, eating processed and fast foods is widely believed to kill more people than smoking.

Many people don't understand the link between poor diet and obesity, and how the direct effect of this affects the immune system, and ultimately increases their risk of heart disease, stroke, diabetes, cancer and dementia.

Please keep reading.

How To Boost Your Immune System Through Diet

Let's get something straight – boosting your immune system is not as simple as grabbing the odd apple, or taking a vitamin tablet every day. If you simply do this - but change nothing else about your health and habits - this is highly unlikely to produce any significant benefit. To help your immune system, you need to under-stand the concept of chronic inflammation.

What Is Chronic Inflammation?

Remember the description at the beginning of this chapter about how your immune system works and what it does in your body? Once the immune response is switched on, it starts the process of inflammation. And although this keeps us alive in the face of infection, a chronic inflammatory response in the body is dangerous for overall health. Chronic inflammation is the key underlying mechanism resulting in premature death from cardiovascular disease (heart attacks and strokes), diabetes, cancer and dementia. In chronic inflammation, the release of inflammatory cells causes atherosclerosis - the build-up of fatty plaques which eventually block the arteries, for example, causing a heart attack. These inflammatory cells also inadvertently cause cancer by failing to recognise and destroy other cells - damaged during every day wear and tear - but are now left behind to become early cancer cells. Inflammatory cells interfere with carbohydrate and fat metabolism leading to diabetes and exacerbating weight gain.

Bad News - Chronic inflammation is a silent killer and unchecked, it has a significant effect on your immune function. It's happening inside our bodies, but none of us realises what's going on.

Obesity is a direct cause of chronic inflammation. This is because hormones produced in adipose tissue set off the inflammatory cascade. Rates of obesity are at epidemic levels.

Here Are Two Key Messages -

- To reduce chronic inflammation, you need to lose weight.
- Weight loss is the most important tool available to boost your immune system.

Good news! - However, this does not mean starvation or working yourself to death in an expensive gym. You can do this by simply changing your diet to eat healthy nutritious food and increasing physical exercise as part of your daily routine. You just need motivation and determination! You really can switch off the production of inflammatory markers and cytokines, which are damaging your tissues every day by making significant changes to your diet. This will also result in losing weight.

Antioxidants

Have you heard of antioxidants? These are clever molecules which 'switch off' chronic inflammation. They are found in many foods but notably in fruit and vegetables. To increase your intake of antioxidants, all you need is to eat a regular, balanced diet, containing an abundance of antioxidant-rich foods. Can't I just take an antioxidant tablet? I'm afraid that studies looking at the longer-term effects of taking antioxidant supplements have failed to show a significant benefit in humans. This is something which continues to puzzle scientists. You are strongly recommended to increase your antioxidant intake by making improvements to your diet.

How To Reduce Chronic Inflammation

There are other ways to reduce chronic inflammation. Measures such as stopping smoking, reducing alcohol consumption, increasing the amount of physical exercise, and getting enough sleep are also very important. However, in this chapter, the focus is on changing your diet.

A Healthy Diet

Eating the wrong foods has a dramatic effect on your health. What are the right foods? What should you be eating? Whichever diet you choose to follow, medical evidence suggests -

- **Reduce Red Meat** - especially processed meat e.g. salami, ham, sausages, bacon, and pre-cooked meats.
- **Adopt A Plant-Based Diet**. You do not necessarily have to become vegetarian or vegan but try to increase the quantity of plants and vegetables in your diet.
- **Reduce Your Intake Of Refined Carbohydrates** e.g. white flour, bread, pasta, pizza dough, and puddings. Very low carbohydrate diets (VLCD's) have proved very successful especially for diabetics or those with pre-diabetes. Limiting glucose consumption leads to fat breakdown.
- **Reduce Your Intake Of Saturated Fats** e.g. butter, cream, cheese, meat, chocolate, biscuits and pastries. Swap to unsaturated fats instead e.g. olive oil, rapeseed oil, avocado, almonds, walnuts, peanuts and oily fish.
- **Restrict Calorie Intake** - Calorie restriction has numerous health benefits. For example, in one 2015 study, those who restricted

their daily calorie consumption by 12% for 2 years had a 10% reduction in body weight and significant health improvements.

- **Eat More Foods With A Low Glycaemic Index** - The glycaemic index is a measure of how quickly sugar is released from food after eating. Foods with a high glycaemic index are sugary foods and drinks, white bread, white rice and pasta. These give a rapid spike in glucose levels and as they fall, you feel hungry again. Low glycaemic foods release sugar slowly so you feel fuller for longer. Low glycaemic foods include many fruits and vegetables, wholemeal grains, pulses and oats.

- **Increase Your Intake Of Dietary Fibre** - Fibre is very important as it bulks out the stool, improving intestinal transport. It also helps you feel full and lowers cholesterol. Fibre is found in whole grains, fruit and vegetables, potatoes in their jackets, and oats, for example,

- **Reduce The Amount Of Salt In Your Diet** –2.5 million deaths a year could be prevented around the world by cutting the amount of salt in the diet to the recommended level (WHO). Salt is found in processed foods e.g. bacon, salami, soy sauce, salty snacks, instant noodles and stock cubes.

- **Consider Going Longer Without Eating** - Fasting – There has been much interest in the effects of fasting on weight loss and health.

- After 8 hours of not eating, your liver has used up its stores of glucose and your body starts to break down fat. This is the basis of the 5:2 and the 16:8 diets.

What Is The Healthiest Diet?

The jury is still out on which diet is best to lose weight, keep it off, and maintain optimal health.

However, the principles are 2-fold:

- **Restrict calorie intake**
- **Increase physical exercise**

Your diet needs to be interesting, varied and satisfying, to enable you to stick to it long-term. This will differ according to personal taste and preference. One popular diet which ticks all these boxes is **The Mediterranean Diet**:

The principles of the Mediterranean Diet are very similar to the current American dietary guidelines issued by the USDA:

https://health.gov/sites/default/files/2019-09/2015-2020_Dietary_Guidelines.pdf Focus on high-quality foods and smaller portions.

Take a look at **The Healthy Plate:**

https://www.hsph.harvard.edu/nutritionsource/healthy-eating-plate/.

Half of your plate should be made up of fruit and vegetables. One-quarter of your plate should be protein. The other quarter should consist of whole grains.

The Mediterranean Diet

The Mediterranean Diet has been the traditional diet of people who for generations, have lived around the Mediterranean Sea. The diet contains a large amount of fruit and vegetables, nuts, seeds and whole grains, with small amounts of lean meat, plus chicken and fish, and unsaturated fats such as olive oil. The Mediterranean Diet has is regarded as 'the gold standard' in preventive medicine, to quote a 2016 discussion paper in the Journal, *Current Opinion in Clinical Nutrition and Metabolic Care*. There is now a huge amount of evidence supporting the health benefits of this diet.

It is associated with lower risks of cardiovascular disease (strokes and heart attacks), heart failure, death and disability. This is because the diet is complete in terms of micronutrients and rich in antioxidants and which have potent anti-inflammatory properties. The *Journal of Public Health and Nutrition* published a 2014 meta-analysis of prospective studies including over 4 million people, looking at the health benefits of the Mediterranean

Diet. The authors concluded that for every 2 point score of adherence to the diet, there was an 8% reduction in all-cause mortality, a 10% reduction in death from cardiovascular disease and a 4% reduction is cancer. https://pubmed.ncbi.nlm.nih.gov/24476641/?dopt=Abstract

A 2017 study in the *Journal of Nutrition* concluded that the Mediterranean Diet was associated with a 13% reduction in the development of type 2 diabetes.

The authors found that people following a diet high in 'unhealthy foods' e.g. red meat, processed foods, refined sugars and fat, were 44% more likely to develop type 2 diabetes. This compared to those eating a 'healthy foods,' e.g. white meat, fish, vegetables, fruits and whole grains, who reduced their risk of developing type-2 diabetes by 16%.

For more information - The Mediterranean Diet:

What is the Mediterranean Diet?   (https://www.nhs.uk/)

Plant-Based Diets

Plant-based diets are increasing in popularity. In the USA, according to one American Consumer Report, between 2014 - 2017 the numbers of vegans increased from 1% to 6%. In the UK, the Vegan Society website states that numbers have quadrupled between 2014 and 2019, with just over 1% of the population now vegan. Plant-based diets appear to offer significant health benefits. Adherence to the diet reduces obesity-related metabolic syndrome and leads to a reduction in chronic inflammation.

For example, in 2017, a paper in the journal *Nutrients* reviewed all the good quality, medical literature, published between 1980 - 2016. Being vegetarian reduced the risk of diabetes by around 30%

Advantages Of A Plant-Based Diet

- Plant-based foods have anti-inflammatory effects. For example, carotenoids and flavonoids found in fruit and vegetables are powerful antioxidants. Carotenoids are found in fruit and vegetables with bright orange or yellow pigments such as carrots, squash, and yellow peppers. Flavonoids are found in onions, broccoli, kale, berries, grapes, tea and lettuce.
- Eating a plant-based diet means you are not eating any meat. The 2018 American Institute for Cancer Research report warns that cooking red meat leads to the production of heterocyclic amines and polycyclic hydrocarbons which have been linked to the development of colorectal cancer. High levels of haem iron in meat can also stimulate the development of cancer cells.

- The plant-based diet includes high levels of phytochemicals, which includes Vitamin C, for example – a powerful antioxidant, and a vital co-factor for many of the pathways involved in the immune response.

Vegan Diet Or Vegetarian Diet?

It's been impossible to say, hand over heart, that the vegan diet is the most beneficial. The vegan diet results in a lower intake of saturated fatty acids, which is good for health, and in addition, an increased intake of fibre, magnesium, iron, ferritin, vitamin B1, C and E. However, vegans have a lower intake of essential vitamins such as B12, D, calcium, zinc and protein.

Benefits Of Increasing Dietary Fibre - A huge 2019 review, looking at 135 million years of personal data, concluded that increasing fibre intake to the greatest intake of 25-29 g per day, resulted in a 15-30% reduction in death from all causes – including heart disease, type 3 diabetes and bowel cancer.

Lower Levels Of Vitamin B12 – However, 50% of vegans have been found to have low levels of vitamin B12 which can have serious health consequences. Low B12 levels are associated with elevated homocysteine levels, and these are a marker for increased atherosclerosis, the major cause of coronary heart disease. Low B12 levels are also linked to stroke, Alzheimer's and Parkinson's disease.

Anaemia - Iron deficient anaemia is also more common in vegans and vegetarian. This causes extreme fatigue, and if it becomes severe, can affect your heart function, for example. Anaemia is a serious medical condition. The Verdict? - Vegans are recommended to consult their doctors while on a vegan diet and have regular blood tests and vitamin supplements.

What Is A Healthy Diet?

Macronutrients - To be nutritionally complete, you need to eat the correct amount, and the right type, of protein, fat, and carbohydrate, every day – see *Table 1: Healthy Diet Essentials*. **Micronutrients** - Your diet must also contain the correct vitamin and mineral content.

Water-soluble vitamins are those which you absorb from your diet and any excess is excreted. These are vitamins B-1, B-2, B-3, B-5, B-6, B-7, B-9, and B-12, and vitamin C.

Fat-soluble vitamins are stored body fat and in your liver. These are vitamins A, D, E, and K. Your body makes Vitamin D in the skin in sunlight, but all other vitamins must come from the diet.

What's The Right Amount?

Rather than being too concerned about the amount of vitamins in foods, it's preferable to follow a varied diet containing a variety of fresh foods, fruit and vegetables. There should be no need for taking vitamin supplements. Minerals are trace elements which derive from volcanic rock and soil. They form part of your diet when you eat animal produce or a plant food source which has grown outdoors. Essential minerals include calcium, chloride (salt), magnesium, potassium, sodium, chromium, copper, fluoride, iodine, iron, manganese, selenium, and zinc.

For more information - see the Harvard Medical School website: https://www.health.harvard.edu/staying-healthy/the-best-foods-for-vitamins-and-minerals.

If you adopt a healthy diet, for example, The Mediterranean Diet, this contains the correct balance of nutrition, and you can follow the diet easily, knowing your body is getting what it needs. Fad diets are often just that – short term gimmicks which are not sustainable over the longer term and do not often health advantages. Your diet should be varied, interesting and make you feel full after eating. If you eat correctly and take some regular exercise, you will find you feel well and are not hungry. If you need to snack choose fruit or vegetables, not high fat, high sugar snacks which gives you a sugar rush and only make you crave more.

Table 1: Healthy Diet Essentials

	Protein	Fat	Carbohydrate
Adult average daily recommended intake Based on an average of 2000 calories per day	Male 88g Female 64g	No more than 35% daily calorie content from fat. Consume - **less saturated fat*** and **more unsaturated**** i.e. monounsaturated and polyunsaturated fats.	50% daily calorie content should be from carbohydrates – an average 225 - 330 g/day.
Main sources	Meat Fish Eggs Milk Cheese Cereal Cereal products Nuts Pulses Beans Lentils	*Saturated fat e.g. fatty meat, processed foods, butter, cakes, biscuits **Unsaturated fats e.g. olive oil, avocado, fatty fish, almonds, cashews, sesame seeds	Consume **more natural unrefined sugars,*** less **refined sugars.**** *Natural sugars e.g. in fruit and vegetables **Refined sugars e.g. table sugar, honey Starch e.g. bread, potatoes, pasta and rice. Fibre e.g. potatoes with their skins intact, fruits, nuts and vegetables
One adult portion size	100g lean meat, (red and poultry) 140g fish 2 medium eggs 3 tablespoons seeds/nuts	Look at food labels: <3g/100g total fat - low fat <1.5g/100g saturated fat – low in saturated fat	Examples: 1 medium baked potato 1 slice wholemeal bread 2-3 tablespoons rice 2-3 tablespoons pasta
Dietary tip	In any diet maintain the daily intake of protein	Use spray oils, such as olive oil, or measure with a teaspoon when cooking	Choose foods with a low glycaemic index e.g. whole grains, brown rice and pasta, porridge and pulses.

Table 1 – Data from the British Nutrition Society

https://www.nutrition.org.uk/

Superfoods – Why Bother?

Who's heard of superfoods? These are a top priority for healthy eating – here's why.

Although there is no agreed definition of superfoods, these foods have a high nutritional content and offer nutritional advantages over other foods. Many superfoods are fruit or vegetables and are frequently brightly coloured due to their rich natural pigments. In truth, the term 'superfoods' is controversial, as proven research of their health benefits in humans is lacking, however, many nutritionists remain convinced of their dietary advantages.

Harvard Medical School advises that no single food can provide all the nutrition one person needs. Food should be eaten from all different good groups. They recommend that healthy dietary eating patterns can reduce the risk of high blood pressure, diabetes and cancer. The medical school specifically endorses the Mediterranean Diet. They stress the importance of including superfoods in your diet saying: "**Superfoods should be singled out for special recognition as they offer important nutrition, can 'power-pack' your meals and snacks, and further enhance your eating pattern.**"

Eating foods packed full of antioxidants is the best way to support your immune system. Now is the best time to look critically at your diet and to think about how you can improve it. You can ♥ start making superfoods a regular part of your daily diet.

For a list of superfoods see *Table 2*: **Love your superfoods!**

Love your superfoods!

This list is not exhaustive – there are simply too many superfoods – virtually all fruit and vegetables with bright colours – are superfoods.

Fruit & Berries	Cruciferous vegetables	Root vegetables	Herbs and Spices	Seeds	Wholegrains
Blueberries	Broccoli	Garlic	Ginger	Chia	Oats
Cranberries	Brussels sprouts	Sweet potato	Turmeric	Flax	Whole wheat
Goji berries	Cabbage	Onion	Basil	Hemp	Bulgar wheat
Strawberries	Kale	Beetroot	Rosemary	Cocoa	Rye
Raspberries	Cauliflower	Radish	Cinnamon	Coffee beans	Millet
Melon	Arugula	Turnip	Cloves	Sesame	Barley
Pineapple		Fennel	Coriander	Pumpkin	Spelt
Kiwi fruit	**Leafy green vegetables**	Carrot	Dill	Sunflower	Quinoa
Avocado	Spinach	Celeriac	Parsley		Brown rice
Pomegranate	Lettuce		Chives		Corn
Pumpkin	Watercress				
Chilli peppers	Endive				
Tomatoes					
Butternut squash					
Cucumber					

Nuts	Unsaturated oils	Fish e.g. oily fish	Meat	Legumes (peas/beans)	Other
Almonds	Olive oil	Salmon	Chicken	Soy	Honey
Walnuts	Sunflower oil	Sardines	Turkey	Mung	Bee pollen
Pistachio	Rapeseed oil	Mackerel		Cannellini	Algae e.g.
Brazils	Vegetable oil	(Any fish or seafood is a superfood)	Lean cuts of; Beef	Pinto	Spirulina, Chlorella
Cashews			Pork	Black-eye	
Hazelnuts	**Coconut oil contains 86% saturated fat – more than butter – and is not a superfood!	*Limit fish containing high levels of mercury e.g. swordfish, shark and fresh tuna	Lamb	Chickpeas	
				Lentils	
			Eggs	Peanuts	
			Chicken egg		
			Duck egg		
			Goose egg		
			Quail e.g.		

*Mercury levels in fish 2019 FDA https://www.fda.gov/food/consumers/advice-about-eating-fish

*Mercury levels in fish 2019:
FDA https://www.fda.gov/food/consumers/advice-about-eating-fish
** Is Coconut Oil A Superfood? - BBC https://www.bbc.co.uk/news/health-42608071

What You Need To Know About Superfoods - At A Glance:

1. **Steam Veggies In A Microwave**:

Don't over boil them. Roasting maintains nutrition but it can deteriorate with the length of cooking. Do not fry them or cover them with butter or salt!

https://www.myfooddiary.com/blog/healthiest-ways-to-cook-vegetables

2. **Fresh Produce:** Eat fresh when possible, however, there is excellent nutritional value eating fruit and vegetables, canned or frozen. However, look for products canned in water for example, with no added salt, and fruits in natural juice, with no added sugar.

https://www.ncbi.nlm.nih.gov/pmc/articles/PMC3649719/

3. **Check A Portion Size Guide**. For example - an average baked potato should be the size of your fist. One portion of fruit is one piece of fruit or one cupful of produce.

https://www.ncbi.nlm.nih.gov/pmc/articles/PMC3649719/

4. **No Fruit Juice.** The sugar content of fruit juices tends to be very high. Eat an orange instead! A lot of the nutrition – including the fibre - is in the pulp of the orange. This is also much more filling.

https://www.diabetes.org.uk/guide-to-diabetes/enjoy-food/what-to-drink-with-diabetes/fruit-juices-and-smoothies

5. **Raw Fruit And Vegetables** have the highest nutritional content. https://www.medicalnewstoday.com/articles/7381

6. **Buy Organic?** - Although there may be advantages to buying organic foods, a huge review of the literature looking at over 50,000 studies failed to confirm a nutritional benefit from organic food. Undoubtedly there are ethical and holistic reasons to support organic farming. However, at the moment it's beyond everybody's pocket. Try to buy local produce which has not had far to travel, store it properly and wash well before use. https://academic.oup.com/ajcn/article/90/3/680/4597089

7. **Benefits Of Milk.** Many people believe cow's milk is a superfood. It contains large quantities of conjugated linoleic acid – a healthy trans fat (as opposed to unhealthy industrial produced trans fats) with powerful anti-oxidant properties. Also, Vitamin A, vitamin E and co-enzyme Q.

https://milkgenomics.org/article/ultimate-superfood-milk-offers-glass-full-antioxidants/

Plant-based milks offer similar nutritional content but don't score so well on taste. It's counterproductive to switch from cow's milk and then need to add sugar to your milk to make it palatable!
https://www.health.harvard.edu/staying-healthy/plant-milk-or-cows-milk-which-is-better-for-you

8. **Chicken Is A Superfood** – a good quality chicken breast contains more protein than beef and much less fat. It does not contain carbohydrates, trans-fats and is low in salt. Try substituting red meat for chicken in your diet.

https://www.chicken.ca/health/v/new-study-confirms-chicken-as-the-latest-superfood

9. **You Will Feel Full After Meals** if you: choose more protein, eat slowly and chew your food, drink water with meals, and don't eat in front of the TV – because being distracted takes your mind off what you are doing. Always have a large portion of low-density superfoods foods on your plate – fruit and vegetables – to fill you up.

10. **Eat Soup!** - Many studies have shown soup is an excellent way to fill you up, reduce overall calorie intake and eat more superfoods! Have a go at making your own?

https://www.ncbi.nlm.nih.gov/pmc/articles/PMC2128765/

Superfoods List - What are the superfoods?   Take a look at

Table 2 - **Love   Your Superfoods**

It's impossible to list all the superfoods! I've had to pick out just a few. Here's a summary below:

Fruits And Berries

Fruits are full of antioxidants, vitamins and minerals, natural sugars and fibre. All fruits and berries are superfoods.

Blueberries are packed with phytonutrients. Their bright colour is due to anthocyanin pigments - flavonoids with potent anti-inflammatory and antioxidant properties.

A 2020 review in the *Journal of Advanced Nutrition* reported regularly eating blueberries is associated with a lower risk of cardiovascular disease, type 2 diabetes, and death. They also help with weight management.

Cranberries are unique in that they contain A-type proanthocyanidin (PAC), which has mild antibacterial effects. Cranberry juice has been used in women with urinary tract infections, although the medical benefits are unproven. American cranberries are rich in polyphenols, which also have antioxidant, and anti-carcinogenic properties. Eating cranberries have shown favourable effects on blood pressure, cholesterol and arterial wall function, although this has not been so far, been proven to reduce the overall risk of heart disease.

Goji berries are bright orange or red berries found in Asia. They are often dried and made into soups, herbal teas, wine or juice. They are full of carotenoids, and flavonoids which are powerful antioxidants. They may help protect the retina in patients with diabetic retinopathy. Rats, fed Gogi berry extract for 10 days, had significantly lower blood glucose levels. Moreover, Gogi berries support body defence mechanisms and may slow the growth of cancer cells.

Strawberries contain ellagic acid, and flavonoids such as anthocyanin, catechin, quercetin and kaempferol. They are highly potent antioxidants. Strawberries have positive effects on the cardiovascular system and lipids. For example - In a 2008 study of patients with cardiovascular risk factors, strawberry puree, eaten along with other berries, was shown to significantly increase HDL cholesterol and lower blood pressure. In a 2010 randomised controlled trial, 30 obese subjects with metabolic syndrome were randomised to eat strawberries - either 50 g freeze-dried strawberries or 3 cups fresh strawberries per day - or drink 4 cups of water (control group), for 8 weeks. Those in the strawberry group demonstrated significantly lower levels of LDL cholesterol.

Chili Peppers – Did you know these are actually fruits? Capsaicin is the major ingredient of chilli. A 2017 study in the journal *PLOS one* surveyed the dietary intake of red hot chilli pepper in 16,719 participants. The authors found mortality was reduced by 13 % in those who regularly ate red hot chilli peppers.

Although the reasons for this are not well understood, it is thought that capsaicin results in increased fat breakdown, promote heat production and facilitates weight loss. It also has antibacterial properties within the gut as well as potent anti-tumour effects.

Cruciferous Vegetables

Love your sprouts! Many people grimace when asked to eat sprouts – but they are vegetables which do you the world of good! Kale, cauliflower, broccoli and sprouts contain chemical compounds – called glucosinolates - which are toxic to early cancer cells. Sorry folks - American dietary guidelines do currently recommend regular consumption of these leafy, green vegetables!

Root Vegetables

Let's consider garlic, for example:-

Garlic – A bulb of garlic contains fibre, lipids, and vitamins A and C, but also two specific sulphur compounds. When a bulb of garlic is crushed it releases a sulphur compound called alliin. This is activated by the enzyme allynase to produce allicin. It is allicin which gives garlic it's characteristic smell and taste. Garlic has been shown to lower blood pressure, reduce cholesterol, increase fibrinolysis and may help reduce thrombosis (blood clots). In 1990 the US National Cancer Institute stated, 'garlic may be the most potent food to have anti-cancer preventative properties.'

Spices

Ginger and turmeric are superfoods of specific interest: **Ginger** – This rhizome is traditionally used in Chinese herbal medicine. It contains a wide range of compounds beneficial to health. The unique taste of ginger comes from the presence of sesquiterpene and monoterpenoid hydrocarbons. Ginger has major anti-inflammatory properties. It's a potent inhibitor of oxidative stress, and has protective effects on the cardiovascular system, and for diabetes and cancer. It can reduce nausea and vomiting, and also prevent muscle pain after exercise.

Turmeric - Also a rhizome and from the ginger family, turmeric contains curcumin, a polyphenol which has strong antioxidant and anti-inflammatory properties. It has a potent action to counteract chronic inflammation. There are several studies in humans, supporting the beneficial effects of curcumin. For example, it's been shown to reduce the levels of pro-inflammatory cytokines. The effects are complex and far-reaching. However, research does suggest there may be a therapeutic role for curcumin in treating metabolic syndrome, arthritis, anxiety and high cholesterol.

Seeds Wholegrains, cocoa, nuts, legumes (beans), coffee beans and oils – most oils derive from seeds – make up the seed category. Seeds have been part of the palaeolithic – 'hunter-gatherer diet' for centuries. Historically these are people who lived off the land on a diet of fresh meat, plants and seeds – whatever they could forage. Nuts and seeds made up a quarter of the diet!

Seeds offer specific nutritional benefits. For example:

Chia seeds derive from the herbaceous plant *Salvia Hispanic* which produces a fruit containing tiny seeds - called Chia seeds. The American Dietetic Association classes Chia seeds as 'bioactive foods' – these are 'foods which have nutritional components which enhance, inhibit or modify, physiologic or metabolic functions' (Biesalski 2009). Chia seeds are often found in muesli, or as thickeners in milkshakes or soups. Chia seeds have a high ratio of omega-6 to omega-3 fatty acids. They are also full of protein phosphorus, calcium and magnesium, vitamins B1 and B2. They are potent antioxidants, with an Oxygen Radical Absorbance (ORAC) capacity the same as hazelnuts and prunes.

Flax Seeds are a food crop grown in the Canadian prairies. Flax seeds produce oil – linseed oil, which are a brownish-red in colour. They can be ground and made into flour. Flax seeds have a high content of ω-3 α-linolenic acid (an essential omega – 3 polyunsaturated fatty acid), fibre, and also lignans - which are plant-based estrogens. Flax seeds have strong antioxidant properties. They have health benefits for cardiovascular disease, high blood pressure, cancer, osteoporosis, autoimmune diseases and more. They are also used by women to help reduce menopausal symptoms.

Hemp Seeds derive from the plant Cannabis sativa. There are two types of this plant – the first type is Marijuana which is well known to have psychoactive properties and is illegal. However, the second type does not have psychoactive properties and is safe to eat. Hemp seeds are full of micronutrients – they are high in protein - containing all nine essential amino acids – and are also high in fibre. They are of specific of interest because they have a high content of omega-3 and of omega- 6 fatty acids.

Cocoa – In fact, a cacao bean is a seed – not a bean! The beans of the Theobroma cacao tree – cocoa beans – are consumed as chocolate all around the world. Cacao is a superfood, but when it's made into chocolate, this contains high levels of saturated fat and sugar – exactly what we should not be eating! In an excellent 2011 review '**Cocoa, Chocolate and Human Health'**, published in the journal *Antioxidants and Redox Signalling*, the authors reported some fascinating findings. Cacao contains high levels of phenolic antioxidants such as flavonoids and procyanidins. The flavonoid epicatechin has favourable effects on the endothelium of blood vessel walls, primarily because of its effect to facilitate local production of nitric oxide. Dark chocolate contains 30%-70% cocoa solids, whereas milk chocolate only contains 7%-15%. Milk chocolate tends to have higher levels of saturated fat and sugar. Dark chocolate contains high levels of magnesium, important for protein synthesis. Also, copper, important for brain growth and development, and potassium, important for heart health.

Studies of how cacao affects the human immune system have not been conducted, however in rats and mice, cacao has been shown to modulate the acute immune response by reducing the production of TNF-α, reducing NO production from macrophages and modifying the neutrophil response in inflammation.
https://www.ncbi.nlm.nih.gov/pmc/articles/PMC3671179/
In his book - Eat Chocolate, Lose Weight - Will Clover PhD, claims that eating dark chocolate 20 minutes before meals, and 5 minutes after, will curb your appetite by 50%!

Coffee - A coffee bean is actually a seed – not a bean! Coffee has been found to have significant antioxidant properties, antibacterial and anti-cancer properties. It contains a high concentration of plant phenols. A 2017 meta-analysis of 127 studies published in the *Annual Review of Nutrition* concluded that coffee was associated with a reduced incidence of breast, colon and prostate cancer, for example, as well as a reduction in cardiovascular disease and reduced overall mortality. However, there was also a higher risk of stomach and lung cancer, and a possible detrimental effect on cholesterol, although the authors felt this was more likely to be influenced by smoking.

Whole Grains

A whole grain contains the endosperm, the germ and the bran. The outer portion is full of fibre, and the kernel in the centre is full of vitamins and minerals. During the refining process, the outer germ and bran are removed, leaving the endosperm only. This is why white flour has less nutritional content than wholemeal or brown flour. There is some evidence that regular consumption may reduce the risks of cardiovascular disease, type-2 diabetes, bowel, pancreatic and stomach cancers.

Nuts - A nut is in fact, a seed encased in a hard shell. Nuts have many characteristics which can benefit human health. In a 2017 review in the journal *Nutrients*, the authors reviewed the health benefits of a range of different nuts for humans. Nuts contain monounsaturated and polyunsaturated fatty acids, high levels of protein and fibre and are a good source of vitamins E and K. They are also full of the minerals copper, magnesium, potassium and selenium. They have potent antioxidant properties as they contain large amounts of carotenoids and other phytochemicals.

- **Almonds** – in one study of participants at high risk of type 2 diabetes, taking 43g per day of almonds as snacks throughout the day for 4 weeks, reduced the feeling of hunger and also blood glucose concentrations. Interestingly study subjects did not gain weight throughout the study. In a further study, eating 60 g of almonds per day for 10 weeks did not result in weight gain either!

- **Walnuts** may be useful in reducing visceral fat. High levels of visceral fat are associated with low concentrations of adiponectin – a hormone involved in regulating glucose levels and breaking down fat. In one small study, eating 48g walnuts per day for 4 days increased adiponectin levels by 15%, as well as showing significant improvements in their lipid profile.

- **Pistachios** have been shown to have health benefits for diabetics. In one study, diabetics eating two snacks a day of 25 g pistachios, had a significant reduction in glycosylated haemoglobin (a marker of diabetic control) and fasting blood glucose.

Legumes are different types of beans. However, they are in the category of seeds because they are the fruits of plants that grow in pods. Beans are full of protein and fibre, rich in B vitamins, and minerals such as iron, copper, magnesium and zinc. A meta-analysis of ten prospective studies concluded that eating legumes for 3 weeks, significantly reduced total cholesterol and LDL cholesterol. Studies in diabetics have shown a regular intake of legumes can lower blood pressure and help improve blood sugars. Adults who regularly eat legumes have a lower body weight than those who do not. Legumes are an integral part of the Mediterranean Diet.

Olive Oil

Olive oil is a healthy, 'unsaturated' fat. It is extracted from olives by a process of crushing or pressing the fruit of the olive itself – not the seed in the middle. The refining process removes a lot of the fruit pulp from the oil but in doing so, also removes the potential health benefits. The most nutritious olive oil is unrefined - Extra Virgin Olive oil – which contains the highest concentration of polyphenols. 98-99% of olive oil is made up of triacylglycerols (TGA's). This is mostly monounsaturated oleic acid, but also palmitic, stearic and linoleic oils. It is packed full of other phytonutrients including phenolic acids, lignans and flavonoids.

The vast majority of studies about health and olive oil have been done in animals, but experts are confident many of these health benefits are seen in humans too. Olive oil has strong antioxidant properties. For example, polyphenols reduce levels of cytokines such as TNF-α, arachidonic acid, IL-6, NF-kB and PEG-2 – all markers of chronic inflammation. One of the key phenolic acids in olive oil is called hydroxytyrosol (HT), has been shown to stimulate mitochondrial biosynthesis, and may offer specific benefits to people with diabetes in whom mitochondrial synthesis is reduced.

Fish

Fish is an important part of a healthy diet, especially for your heart. It's a rich source of protein and omega-3 fatty acids (eicosapentaenoic acid (EPA) and docosahexaenoic acid (DH), vitamin D, iodine and selenium. Oily fish such as salmon, mackerel or sardines contain a particularly high concentration of omega-3 fatty acids. These are essential in the structure and maintenance of the cell wall. They also have a major role in the immune response, for example, to reduce the production of proinflammatory cytokines. They are also involved in fat storage and metabolism.

Omega-3 is most beneficial when obtained from the diet rather than tablet supplementation.

Vitamin D is formed naturally in the skin in sunlight. However, levels of vitamin D are often low especially in the winter when the days are short.

Low vitamin D levels are associated with metabolic syndrome and obesity. Fish is the only other natural source of vitamin D.

Fish contains high levels of iodine and selenium - both essential for normal thyroid function. People with metabolic syndrome, tend to have higher thyroid volumes. American FDA guidelines recommend eating 8 oz of fish/shellfish, 2-3 times per week (2 -3 portions/week).

Egg - The humble egg has much to commend it! Egg contains large amounts of protein, for only a moderate number of calories, and is a rich source of Vitamin A, B12 and iron, zinc and calcium. Eggs are inexpensive and versatile. Egg contains high levels of antioxidants and for example, may reduce oxidative stress in the gut wall. Some of the egg constituents, for example, egg-white pleiotrophin, play a key role in the immune response, helping to prolong lymphocyte survival, and also by signalling white cells to move to the area of and immune attack (chemotaxis).

There has been concern about whether eating too many eggs might raise cholesterol. A very recent study published in the *Journal of the American Medical Association* JAMA March 2020, showed that eating 3-4 eggs per week, as is currently recommended in the US, increased the risk of cardiovascular disease by 6% and death by 8%. However, before you get too worried about this, a major limitation of the study is that the investigators only ask people what they had been eating, from memory.

This may well mean the results were not very accurate. The authors concluded people should not stop eating eggs, but eat them in moderation, and try to reduce cholesterol from their diet, for example by limiting red meat.

The Microbiome And The Immune System

Your gut contains 10 - 100 trillion micro-organisms! These are bacteria, viruses and fungi - which live in and around the lumen of your gut wall. Your body learns to recognise which cells belong to you, which ones can live there happily and which it needs to destroy. Each person on the planet has a different microbiome. At birth, the gut is almost sterile, but this is gradually colonised as the baby feeds by breast or bottle, and then by the introduction of solid food. Throughout life, everyone acquires a different gut flora according to their diet and health.

The constituents of your gut flora have a huge effect on your health. The organisms in the gut wall signal the brain to take specific actions. They also directly stimulate or switch off various biochemical processes. By analysing your faeces, scientists can analyse your microbiome. The constituents of your microbiome have a direct effect on the function of your immune system. However, you can make changes to your gut microbiome by making changes to your diet.

The Mediterranean Diet, for example, has been shown to result in alterations to the microbiome, and this is then associated with significant changes in markers of chronic inflammation. In a study published very recently (13th March 2020) in the *New England Journal of Medicine,* 612 frail elderly people were followed by for 12-months before, and then for 12-months after, adopting the Mediterranean Diet.

After the study, the authors found a change in the diversity of organisms within the microbiome, along with an overall improvement in their levels of frailty, and improved cognitive function. They also found significant changes in markers of chronic inflammation such as C-reactive protein and interleukin -17.

There is much yet to be learned about the gut microbiome and its importance for human health. However one fact, which has been clearly established, it that the flora in the gut of an obese person is very different from that of someone who is lean. A comprehensive 2017 review, the authors concluded that making changes to your diet can indeed change your microbiome and result in improvements in health.

Final Thoughts

In this chapter, I've explained the importance of a healthy diet to maintain a healthy immune system and a healthy body. I hope you can see that improving your immune system is not just about eating an occasional apple or swallowing a vitamin pill! It's about improving your general health, and a large part of this comes down to improving your diet. Remember that leanness is correlated with longevity. Don't we all want to live a long life?

When did you last weigh and measure yourself and work out your BMI? If you are facing up to being obese – you are not alone. Isn't it time we all took responsibility for our health and did something about it? COVID-19 marks the time for change. Every situation is an opportunity. We can all emerge from is pandemic healthier and happier if we try. Finding a diet that you can follow which is interesting, delicious and filling is one of nature's wonders. There are so many amazing things you can eat, recipes you can follow and fantastic food experiences that go far beyond reaching for another hot dog!

I want you to stay well during this COVID-19 pandemic, and beyond!

So right now ... I'm off to fix myself a fruit smoothie!

Dr Deborah Lee

About The Author

Sexual And Reproductive Health Specialist, Medical And Healthcare Writer, BM, MFFP, MRCGP, DRCOG, Dip GUM, Dip Colp, LOC Med Ed **GMC no. 3129913**

Dr Deborah Lee has worked for many years in the NHS, mostly as Lead Clinician within an integrated Community Sexual Health Service. She now works as a health and medical writer, with an emphasis on women's health. Dr Lee is a medical content writer for Dr Fox (**Dr Fox Online Pharmacy**).

Dr Lee writes for many **media outlets** including The Sun, The Daily Express, Bella magazine, Red magazine, Cosmopolitan, Net Doctor, and many more. She remains passionate about all aspects of medicine - including obesity, weight loss, diet, and nutrition.

After qualifying from **University of Southampton** Medical School in 1986, Dr Lee trained as a GP and after a number of years specialised in Sexual & Reproductive Health (S&RH).

S&RH is a very broad speciality which includes for example: Gynaecology and Medical Gynaecology, all types and aspects of contraceptive care including coils and implants, dealing with unplanned pregnancies, abnormal smears, screening and treating STIs in both males and females, Young People's Sexual Health, Sexual Assault, and in particular Menopause Care - which has been her special interest. Dr Lee set up and ran her own specialist menopause clinic.

During this time, Dr Lee wrote extensively, and had numerous medical publications, as well as working as sub-editor for a medical journal. She has also written articles for The Huffington Post UK under the pseudonym Dr **Daisy Mae**.

Medical education and training has also been a large part of Dr Lee's professional career. She has been a Contraception & Sexual Health Trainer, a Faculty Examiner and a Training Programme Director.

Dr Deborah Lee/ Dr Daisy Mae

Freelance Health Writer https://healthcarewriterdr.com/services/

- **Dr Daisy's Sexual Health Blog, The Huffington Post**
  https://www.huffingtonpost.co.uk/author/daisy-mae/
- **Dr Daisy Blog, - Menopause Matters**
  https://www.menopausematters.co.uk/daisyblog.php
- **LinkedIn** - www.linkedin.com/in/dr-daisy-mae
- **Twitter- Daisy Mae**

References

For The Following Chapters Within This Title:

Food To Boost The Immune System - By Dr Deborah Lee's

References:

For more information -

- **Dietary Guidelines for Americans 2015-2020 – 8th Edition USDA**
  https://health.gov/sites/default/files/2019-09/2015-2020_Dietary_Guidelines.pdf
- **BMI calculator** https://bmicalculatorusa.com/
- **Find a Nutritionist**
  https://www.nutritionistresource.org.uk/?gclid=CjwKCAjwssD0BRBlEiwA-JP5rLlSdbdRqmgpNlZR_khFW5JuucRwD2pd8f8N7rzACwR8NqWLrG58ZBoC36QQAvD_BwE
- **American Heart Association – Losing Weight**
  https://www.heart.org/en/healthy-living/healthy-eating/losing-weight
- **The Health Sciences Academy Free Starter Course Online**
  https://thehealthsciencesacademy.org/registration-free-starter-nutrition-course/

References

Nutritional Modulation of Immune Function: Analysis of Evidence, Mechanisms, and Clinical Relevance. Front Immunol. 2018; 9: 3160. Published online 2019 Jan 15. doi: 10.3389/fimmu.2018.03160. PMCID: PMC6340979. PMID: 30697214
Nutritional Modulation of Immune Function: Analysis of Evidence, Mechanisms, and Clinical Relevance. Dayong Wu,[1,*] Erin D. Lewis,[1] Munyong Pae,[2] and Simin Nikbin Meydani[1]
https://www.ncbi.nlm.nih.gov/pmc/articles/PMC6340979/

Understanding nutrition and immunity in disease management. Journal of Traditional and Complementary Medicine. Volume 7, Issue 4, October 2017, Pages 386-391

Edwin L.Cooper, Melissa J.May. https://doi.org/10.1016/j.jtcme.2016.12.002
https://www.sciencedirect.com/science/article/pii/S2225411016303029

Gut barrier function in malnourished patients. Gut. 1998 Mar; 42(3): 396–401.doi: 10.1136/gut.42.3.396. PMCID: PMC1727047. PMID: 9577348. F Welsh, S Farmery, K MacLennan, M Sheridan, G Barclay, P Guillou, and J Reynolds
https://www.ncbi.nlm.nih.gov/pmc/articles/PMC1727047/

The Interaction between Nutrition and Infection. Peter Katona, Judit Katona-Apte*Clinical Infectious Diseases*, Volume 46, Issue 10, 15 May 2008, Pages 1582–1588, https://doi.org/10.1086/587658 Published: 15 May 2008
https://academic.oup.com/cid/article/46/10/1582/294025

Feeding America https://www.feedingamerica.org/.
https://www.feedingamerica.org/hunger-in-america/facts

The Hidden Dangers of Fast and Processed Food· Am J Lifestyle Med. 2018 Sep-Oct; 12(5): 375–381. Published online 2018 Apr 3. doi: 10.1177/1559827618766483. PMCID: PMC6146358 PMID: 30283262. Joel Fuhrman, MD

Association of changes in red meat consumption with total and cause-specific mortality among US women and men: two prospective cohort studies. *BMJ* 2019; 365 doi: https://doi.org/10.1136/bmj.l2110 (Published 12 June 2019)Cite this as: BMJ 2019;365:l2110

What is a plant-based diet and why should you try it? POSTED SEPTEMBER 26, 2018, 10:30 AM, UPDATED SEPTEMBER 27, 2018, 12:56 PM Katherine D. McManus, MS, RD, LDN https://www.health.harvard.edu/blog/what-is-a-plant-based-diet-and-why-should-you-try-it-2018092614760

Overweight and diabetes prevention: is a low-carbohydrate–high-fat diet recommendable? Eur J Nutr. 2018; 57(4): 1301–1312.Fred Brouns. Published

online 2018 Mar 14. doi: 10.1007/s00394-018-1636-yPMCID: PMC5959976.
PMID: 29541907   https://www.ncbi.nlm.nih.gov/pmc/articles/PMC5959976/

Fat: The Facts. NHS Eat Well https://www.nhs.uk/live-well/eat-well/different-fats-nutrition/

2 years of calorie restriction and cardiometabolic risk (CALERIE): exploratory outcomes of a multicentre, phase 2, randomised controlled trial. Kraus WE, et al *Lancet Diabetes and Endocrinology.* 2019 July 11. doi: 10.1016/S2213-8587(19)30151-2. [Epub ahead of print].

Does the Interdependence between Oxidative Stress and Inflammation Explain the Antioxidant Paradox? Oxid Med Cell Longev. 2016; 2016: 5698931. Published online 2016 Jan 5. doi: 10.1155/2016/5698931 PMCID: PMC4736408 PMID: 26881031. Subrata Kumar Biswas[*]

https://www.ncbi.nlm.nih.gov/pmc/articles/PMC4736408/

NHS Choices: What is the glycaemic index? https://www.nhs.uk/common-health-questions/food-and-diet/what-is-the-glycaemic-index-gi/

British Nutrition Foundation – Dietary Fibre
https://www.nutrition.org.uk/healthyliving/basics/fibre.html

World Health Organisation - Salt Reduction
https://www.who.int/news-room/fact-sheets/detail/salt-reduction

Harvard School of Public Health, The Healthy eating Plate -
https://www.hsph.harvard.edu/nutritionsource/healthy-eating-plate/

Mediterranean diet and life expectancy; beyond olive oil, fruits and vegetables. Curr Opin Clin Nutr Metab Care. Author manuscript; available in PMC 2018 Apr 17. Published in final edited form as: Curr Opin Clin Nutr Metab Care. 2016 Nov; 19(6): 401–407. doi: 10.1097/MCO.0000000000000316. PMCID: PMC5902736. NIHMSID: NIHMS939601
PMID: 27552476. Miguel A. Martinez-Gonzalez[1,2] and Nerea Martín-Calvo[1,2]
https://www.ncbi.nlm.nih.gov/pmc/articles/PMC5902736/

Mediterranean Diet and Health Status: An Updated Meta-Analysis and a Proposal for a Literature-Based Adherence Score Public Health Nutr, 17 (12), 2769-82 Dec 2014
Francesco Sofi [1], Claudio Macchi [2], Rosanna Abbate [1], Gian Franco Gensini [1], Alessandro Casini [1] PMID: 24476641 DOI: 10.1017/S1368980013003169
https://pubmed.ncbi.nlm.nih.gov/24476641/?dopt=Abstract

Dietary Patterns and Type 2 Diabetes: A Systematic Literature Review and Meta-Analysis of Prospective Studies Franziska Jannasch, Janine Kröger, Matthias B Schulze   *The Journal of Nutrition*, Volume 147, Issue 6, June 2017, Pages 1174–1182, https://doi.org/10.3945/jn.116.242552 Published: 19 April 2017
https://academic.oup.com/jn/article/147/6/1174/4630426?ijkey=bb2d628650e989a9a4cdcb6512fe189d503f5fc5&keytype2=tf_ipsecsha

Adherence to a Vegetarian Diet and Diabetes Risk: A Systematic Review and Meta-Analysis of Observational Studies by Yujin Lee and Kyong Park Department of Food and Nutrition, Yeungnam University, Gyeongsan 38541, Gyeongbuk, Korea. *Nutrients* 2017, *9*(6), 603; https://doi.org/10.3390/nu9060603. Received: 11 May 2017 / Revised: 7 June 2017 / Accepted: 10 June 2017 / Published: 14 June 2017
https://www.mdpi.com/2072-6643/9/6/603/htm

Top Trends in Prepared Foods 2017: Exploring trends in meat, fish and seafood; pasta, noodles and rice; prepared meals; savory deli food; soup; and meat substitutes. June 2017 Report ID: 4959853 • Format: PDF
https://www.reportbuyer.com/product/4959853/top-trends-in-prepared-foods-2017-exploring-trends-in-meat-fish-and-seafood-pasta-noodles-and-rice-prepared-meals-savory-deli-food-soup-and-meat-substitutes.html

The Vegan Society   https://www.vegansociety.com/news/media/statistics

Effect of the Anti-Inflammatory Diet in People with Diabetes and Pre-Diabetes: A Randomized Controlled Feeding Study. J Restor Med. Author manuscript; available in PMC 2019 Jun 5.

Published in final edited form as: J Restor Med. 2019; 8(1): e20190107.

Published online 2019 Feb 15. doi: 10.14200/jrm.2019.0107 PMCID: PMC6550471

NIHMSID: NIHMS1020614 PMID: 31179163 . Heather Zwickey, PhD,[a,*] Angela Horgan, PhD, RD, LD,[b] Doug Hanes, PhD,[a] Heather Schiffke, MATCM, Annie Moore,

MD, MBA,[c] Helané Wahbeh, ND, MCR,[a] Julia Jordan, MS, RD, LD,[b] Lila Ojeda, MS, RDN,[b] Martha McMurry,[b] Patricia Elmer, PhD,[a,§] and Jonathan Q Purnell, MD[b]
https://www.ncbi.nlm.nih.gov/pmc/articles/PMC6550471/

American Institute for Cancer Research. About the Third Expert Report. Diet, Nutrition, Physical Activity and Cancer: a Global Perspective.
https://www.wcrf.org/sites/default/files/Meat-Fish-and-Dairy-products.pdf
Vitamin C and Immune Function Nutrients. 2017 Nov; 9(11): 1211. Published online 2017 Nov 3. doi: 10.3390/nu9111211. PMCID: PMC5707683. PMID: 29099763. Anitra C. Carr[1,*] and Silvia Maggini[2]
https://www.ncbi.nlm.nih.gov/pmc/articles/PMC5707683
The effects of plant-based diets on the body and the brain: a systematic review. Transl Psychiatry. 2019; 9: 226. Published online 2019 Sep 12. doi: 10.1038/s41398-019-0552-0
PMCID: PMC6742661 PMID: 31515473. Evelyn Medawar,[✉,1,2,3] Sebastian Huhn,[4] Arno Villringer,[1,2,3] and A. Veronica Witte[1]
https://www.ncbi.nlm.nih.gov/pmc/articles/PMC6742661/#CR57
British Nutrition Society – Protein
https://www.nutrition.org.uk/nutritionscience/nutrients-food-and-ingredients/protein.html?start=2
Effects of Superfoods on Risk Factors of Metabolic Syndrome: A Systematic Review of Human Intervention Trials José J van den Driessche [1], Jogchum Plat [1], Ronald P Mensink [1] PMID: 29557436 DOI: 10.1039/C7FO01792H
https://pubmed.ncbi.nlm.nih.gov/29557436/

Cranberries

Cranberries and Their Bioactive Constituents in Human Health[1,2]. Adv Nutr. 2013 Nov; 4(6): 618–632. Published online 2013 Nov 6. doi: 10.3945/an.113.004473 PMCID: PMC3823508 PMID: 24228191. Jeffrey B. Blumberg,[3,*] Terri A. Camesano,[4] Aedin Cassidy,[5] Penny Kris-Etherton,[6] Amy Howell,[7] Claudine Manach,[8] Luisa M. Ostertag,[5] Helmut Sies,[9] Ann Skulas-Ray,[6] and Joseph A. Vita[10]
https://www.ncbi.nlm.nih.gov/pmc/articles/PMC3823508/

Blueberries

Recent Research on the Health Benefits of Blueberries and Their Anthocyanins Adv Nutr,11 (2), 224-236, 2020 Mar 1 Wilhelmina Kalt [1], Aedin Cassidy [2], Luke R

Howard [3], Robert Krikorian [4], April J Stull [5], Francois Tremblay [6], Raul Zamora-Ros [7] Affiliations expand PMID: 31329250 DOI: 10.1093/advances/nmz065
https://pubmed.ncbi.nlm.nih.gov/31329250/

Gogi berries

Goji Berries as a Potential Natural Antioxidant Medicine: An Insight into Their Molecular Mechanisms of Action. Oxid Med Cell Longev. 2019; 2019: 2437397. Published online 2019 Jan 9. doi: 10.1155/2019/2437397 PMCID: PMC6343173 PMID: 30728882. Zheng Feei Ma,[1,2] Hongxia Zhang, [3] Sue Siang Teh, [3,4] Chee Woon Wang, [5] Yutong Zhang,[6] Frank Hayford, [7] Liuyi Wang, [1] Tong Ma, [8] Zihan Dong, [1] Yan Zhang, [1] and Yifan Zhu [1]
https://www.ncbi.nlm.nih.gov/pmc/articles/PMC6343173/

Strawberries

Favorable Effects of Berry Consumption on Platelet Function, Blood Pressure, and HDL Cholesterol. Randomised Controlled Trial. Am J Clin Nutr, 87 (2), 323-31 Feb 2008. Iris Erlund [1], Raika Koli, Georg Alfthan, Jukka Marniemi, Pauli Puukka, Pirjo Mustonen, Pirjo Mattila, Antti Jula. PMID: 18258621 DOI: 10.1093/ajcn/87.2.323
https://pubmed.ncbi.nlm.nih.gov/18258621/

Strawberries 2

Strawberries decrease atherosclerotic markers in subjects with metabolic syndrome. Nutr Res. Author manuscript; available in PMC 2011 Jul 1. Published in final edited form as:

Nutr Res. 2010 Jul; 30(7): 462–469. doi: 10.1016/j.nutres.2010.06.016 PMCID: PMC2929388 NIHMSID: NIHMS223632 PMID: 20797478 Arpita Basu,[*] Mei Du,[#] Marci Wilkinson,[*] Brandi Simmons,[*] Mingyuan Wu,[#] Nancy M. Betts,[*] Dong Xu Fu,[#] and Timothy J. Lyons[#†]
https://www.ncbi.nlm.nih.gov/pmc/articles/PMC2929388/#R5

Chilli

The Association of Hot Red Chili Pepper Consumption and Mortality: A Large Population-Based Cohort Study. PLoS One. 2017; 12(1): e0169876. Published online 2017 Jan 9. doi: 10.1371/journal.pone.0169876 PMCID: PMC5222470 PMID: 28068423 Mustafa Chopan[*] and Benjamin Littenberg Oreste Gualillo, Editor
https://www.ncbi.nlm.nih.gov/pmc/articles/PMC5222470/

Garlic

Garlic: a review of potential therapeutic effects. Avicenna J Phytomed. 2014 Jan-Feb; 4(1): 1–14. PMCID: PMC4103721 PMID: 25050296. Leyla Bayan,[1] Peir Hossain

Koulivand,[1] and Ali Gorji[1,2,*]

https://www.ncbi.nlm.nih.gov/pmc/articles/PMC4103721/#B22

Ginger

Anti-Oxidative and Anti-Inflammatory Effects of Ginger in Health and Physical Activity: Review of Current Evidence. Int J Prev Med. 2013 Apr; 4(Suppl 1): S36–S42. PMCID: PMC3665023 PMID: 23717767. Nafiseh Shokri Mashhadi, Reza Ghiasvand,[1,2] Gholamreza Askari,[1,2] Mitra Hariri,[1,2] Leila Darvishi,[1,2] and Mohammad Reza Mofid[3]

https://www.ncbi.nlm.nih.gov/pmc/articles/PMC3665023/

Chia seeds

The Chemical Composition and Nutritional Value of Chia Seeds—Current State of Knowledge. Nutrients. 2019 Jun; 11(6): 1242. Published online 2019 May 31. doi: 10.3390/nu11061242. PMCID: PMC6627181 PMID: 31159190. Bartosz Kulczyński,[1] Joanna Kobus-Cisowska,[1] Maciej Taczanowski,[2] Dominik Kmiecik,[1] and Anna Gramza-Michałowska[1,*]

https://www.ncbi.nlm.nih.gov/pmc/articles/PMC6627181/

Flax seeds

Flax and flaxseed oil: an ancient medicine & modern functional food. J Food Sci Technol. 2014 Sep; 51(9): 1633–1653. Published online 2014 Jan 10. doi: 10.1007/s13197-013-1247-9

PMCID: PMC4152533. PMID: 25190822. Ankit Goyal,[✉] Vivek Sharma, Neelam Upadhyay, Sandeep Gill, and Manvesh Sihag

https://www.ncbi.nlm.nih.gov/pmc/articles/PMC4152533/

Quinoa

Quinoa Seed Lowers Serum Triglycerides in Overweight and Obese Subjects: A Dose-Response Randomized Controlled Clinical Trial. Curr Dev Nutr. 2017 Sep; 1(9): e001321. Published online 2017 Aug 24. doi: 10.3945/cdn.117.001321

PMCID: PMC5998774. PMID: 29955719. Diana Navarro-Perez,[1] Jessica Radcliffe,[2] Audrey Tierney,[2] and Markandeya Jois[1]

https://www.ncbi.nlm.nih.gov/pmc/articles/PMC5998774/#b3

Cocoa

Cocoa and Chocolate in Human Health and Disease. Antioxid Redox Signal. 2011 Nov 15; 15(10): 2779–2811. doi: 10.1089/ars.2010.3697. MCID: PMC4696435.

PMID: 21470061 David L. Katz,[✉] Kim Doughty, and Ather Ali
https://www.ncbi.nlm.nih.gov/pmc/articles/PMC4696435/#B149

National Centre for Complementary and Integrative Health – Acai.
https://www.nccih.nih.gov/health/acai

United States Department of Agriculture – Industrial Hemp.
https://nifa.usda.gov/industrial-hemp

Nuts

Nuts and Human Health Outcomes: A Systematic Review. Nutrients. 2017 Dec; 9(12): 1311. Published online 2017 Dec 2. doi: 10.3390/nu9121311. PMCID: PMC5748761. PMID: 29207471 Rávila Graziany Machado de Souza, Raquel Machado Schincaglia, Gustavo Duarte Pimentel, and João Felipe Mota[*].
https://www.ncbi.nlm.nih.gov/pmc/articles/PMC5748761/

Fish

Nutrients in Fish and Possible Associations with Cardiovascular Disease Risk Factors in Metabolic Syndrome. Nutrients. 2018 Jul; 10(7): 952. Published online 2018 Jul 23. doi: 10.3390/nu10070952 PMCID: PMC6073188. PMID: 30041496 Christine Tørris,[1,*] Milada Cvancarova Småstuen,[1] and Marianne Molin[1,2]
https://www.ncbi.nlm.nih.gov/pmc/articles/PMC6073188/#B88-nutrients-10-00952

Olive oil

Potential Health Benefits of Olive Oil and Plant Polyphenols. Int J Mol Sci. 2018 Mar; 19(3): 686. Published online 2018 Feb 28. doi: 10.3390/ijms19030686. PMCID: PMC5877547. PMID: 29495598. Monika Gorzynik-Debicka,[1,†] Paulina Przychodzen,[1,†] Francesco Cappello,[2,3] Alicja Kuban-Jankowska,[1] Antonella Marino Gammazza,[2,3] Narcyz Knap,[1] Michal Wozniak,[1] and Magdalena Gorska-Ponikowska[1,4,*] https://www.ncbi.nlm.nih.gov/pmc/articles/PMC5877547/

Food

Feeding the Immune System. Proc Nutr Soc. 72 (3), 299-309 Aug 2013 Philip C Calder[1] PMID: 23688939.DOI: 10.1017/S0029665113001286
https://pubmed.ncbi.nlm.nih.gov/23688939/

Whole grains

Health Benefits of Dietary Whole Grains: An Umbrella Review of Meta-analyses. J Chiropr Med. 2017 Mar; 16(1): 10–18. Published online 2016 Nov 18. doi: 10.1016/j.jcm.2016.08.008

PMCID: PMC5310957 PMID: 28228693. Marc P. McRae, MSc, DC, FACN, DACBN

https://www.ncbi.nlm.nih.gov/pmc/articles/PMC5310957/

Recommending superfoods. Harvard Medical School. 10 superfoods to boost a healthy diet. POSTED AUGUST 29, 2018, 10:30 AM. Katherine D. McManus, MS, RD, LDN

https://www.health.harvard.edu/blog/10-superfoods-to-boost-a-healthy-diet-2018082914463

Turmeric

Curcumin: A Review of Its' Effects on Human Health. Foods. 2017 Oct; 6(10): 92. Published online 2017 Oct 22. doi: 10.3390/foods6100092. PMCID: PMC5664031. PMID: 29065496. Susan J. Hewlings[1,2,*] and Douglas S. Kalman[3,4]

https://www.ncbi.nlm.nih.gov/pmc/articles/PMC5664031/#B29-foods-06-00092

Ginger

Anti-Oxidative and Anti-Inflammatory Effects of Ginger in Health and Physical Activity: Review of Current Evidence. Int J Prev Med. 2013 Apr; 4(Suppl 1): S36–S42...PMCID: PMC3665023. PMID: 23717767. Nafiseh Shokri Mashhadi, Reza Ghiasvand,[1,2] Gholamreza Askari,[1,2] Mitra Hariri,[1,2] Leila Darvishi,[1,2] and Mohammad Reza Mofid[3]

https://www.ncbi.nlm.nih.gov/pmc/articles/PMC3665023/

Health benefits of seeds

Consumption of Plant Seeds and Cardiovascular Health: Epidemiologic and Clinical Trial Evidence. Circulation. Author manuscript; available in PMC 2014 Jul 30.

Published in final edited form as: Circulation. 2013 Jul 30; 128(5): 553–565.

doi: 10.1161/CIRCULATIONAHA.112.001119. PMCID: PMC3745769. NIHMSID: NIHMS510316. PMID: 23897849. Emilio Ros, MD, PhD[1] and Frank B. Hu, MD, PhD[2] https://www.ncbi.nlm.nih.gov/pmc/articles/PMC3745769/

Legumes: Health Benefits and Culinary Approaches to Increase Intake. Clin Diabetes. 2015 Oct; 33(4): 198–205. doi: 10.2337/diaclin.33.4.198 PMCID: PMC4608274. PMID: 26487796 Rani Polak,[1] Edward M. Phillips,[1] and Amy Campbell[2]

https://www.ncbi.nlm.nih.gov/pmc/articles/PMC4608274/

Coffee

Coffee, Caffeine, and Health Outcomes: An Umbrella Review. Annual Review of Nutrition. Vol. 37:131-156 (Volume publication date August 2017) Giuseppe Grosso,[1,2] Justyna Godos,[1,3] Fabio Galvano,[3] and Edward L. Giovannucci[4,5,6]
https://www.annualreviews.org/doi/10.1146/annurev-nutr-071816-064941

Cruciferous vegetables

National Cancer Institute. Cruciferous Vegetables and Cancer Prevention
https://www.cancer.gov/about-cancer/causes-prevention/risk/diet/cruciferous-vegetables-fact-sheet

Egg

The Golden Egg: Nutritional Value, Bioactivities, and Emerging Benefits for Human Health. Nutrients. 2019 Mar; 11(3): 684. Published online 2019 Mar 22. doi: 10.3390/nu11030684. PMCID: PMC6470839. PMID: 30909449. Sophie Réhault-Godbert,* Nicolas Guyot, and Yves Nys.
https://www.ncbi.nlm.nih.gov/pmc/articles/PMC6470839/

Northwestern University. "Higher egg and cholesterol consumption hikes heart disease and early death risk." ScienceDaily. ScienceDaily, 15 March 2019. www.sciencedaily.com/releases/2019/03/190315110858.htm

Egg

Associations of Dietary Cholesterol or Egg Consumption with Incident Cardiovascular Disease and Mortality. March 19, 2019. Victor W. Zhong, PhD[1]; Linda Van Horn, PhD[1]; Marilyn C. Cornelis, PhD[1]; et al
https://jamanetwork.com/journals/jama/fullarticle/2728487

The Microbiome

Defining the human microbiome, Luke K Ursell, Jessica L Metcalf, Laura Wegener Parfrey, Rob Knight. Nutrition Reviews, Volume 70, Issue suppl_1, 1 August 2012, Pages S38–S44, https://doi.org/10.1111/j.1753-4887.2012.00493.x Published: 01 August 2012* PMCID: PMC3426293 NIHMSID: NIHMS369735 PMID: 22861806
https://academic.oup.com/nutritionreviews/article/70/suppl_1/S38/1921538

Microbiome in Mediterranean Diet

Ghosh TS, Rampelli S, Jeffery IB, *et al*. Mediterranean diet intervention alters the gut microbiome in older people reducing frailty and improving health status: the NU-AGE 1-year dietary intervention across five European countries. *Gut* Published

Online First: 17 February 2020. doi: 10.1136/gutjnl-2019-319654.
https://gut.bmj.com/content/early/2020/01/31/gutjnl-2019-319654

The microbiome

20 Things You Didn't Know About the Human Gut Microbiome. J Cardiovasc Nurs. Author manuscript; available in PMC 2015 Nov 1. Published in final edited form as: J Cardiovasc Nurs. 2014 Nov-Dec; 29(6): 479–481.
doi: 10.1097/JCN.0000000000000166. PMCID: PMC4191858.
NIHMSID: NIHMS589935. PMID: 25290618
https://www.ncbi.nlm.nih.gov/pmc/articles/PMC4191858/

Influence of diet on the gut microbiome and implications for human health. J Transl Med. 2017; 15: 73. Published online 2017 Apr 8. doi: 10.1186/s12967-017-1175-y PMCID: PMC5385025. PMID: 28388917. Rasnik K. Singh,[1] Hsin-Wen Chang,[2] Di Yan,[2] Kristina M. Lee,[2] Derya Ucmak,[2] Kirsten Wong,[2] Michael Abrouk,[3] Benjamin Farahnik,[4] Mio Nakamura,[2] Tian Hao Zhu,[5] Tina Bhutani,[2] and Wilson Liao[2]
https://www.ncbi.nlm.nih.gov/pmc/articles/PMC5385025/

Studies don't show benefit from antioxidant tablets

Does the Interdependence between Oxidative Stress and Inflammation Explain the Antioxidant Paradox? Oxid Med Cell Longev. 2016; 2016: 5698931. Published online 2016 Jan 5. doi: 10.1155/2016/5698931 PMCID: PMC4736408 PMID: 26881031. Subrata Kumar Biswas
https://www.ncbi.nlm.nih.gov/pmc/articles/PMC4736408/

Benefits of the Mediterranean Diet

Mediterranean Diet and Health Status: An Updated Meta-Analysis and a Proposal for a Literature-Based Adherence Score. Francesco Sofi [1], Claudio Macchi [2], Rosanna Abbate [1], Gian Franco Gensini [1], Alessandro Casini [1]
PMID: 24476641 DOI: 10.1017/S1368980013003169
https://pubmed.ncbi.nlm.nih.gov/24476641/?dopt=Abstract

Effects of the plant-based diet

The effects of plant-based diets on the body and the brain: a systematic review. Transl Psychiatry. 2019; 9: 226. Published online 2019 Sep 12. doi: 10.1038/s41398-019-0552-0. PMCID: PMC6742661. PMID: 31515473. Evelyn Medawar,[1,2,3] Sebastian Huhn,[4] Arno Villringer,[1,2,3] and A. Veronica Witte[1]
https://www.ncbi.nlm.nih.gov/pmc/articles/PMC6742661/#CR57

References:

Yoga as a Therapy: The Healing Power of Yoga to Support your Wellbeing During and After Corona Virus - *By Dr Stephanie Minchin*

Acheson, D. (1998). Inequalities in health: report of an independent inquiry.

Birdee, G. S., Yeh, G. Y., Wayne, P. M., Phillips, R. S., Davis, R. B., & Gardiner, P. (2009). Clinical applications of yoga for the pediatric population: A systematic review. *Academic Pediatrics*, 9(4), 212-220.

Brown, R. P., & Gerbarg, P. L. (2005). Sudarshan Kriya yogic breathing in the treatment of stress, anxiety, and depression: part I—neurophysiologic model. *Journal of Alternative & Complementary Medicine*, 11(1), 189-201.

Büssing, A., Michalsen, A., Khalsa, S. B. S., Telles, S., & Sherman, K. J. (2012). Effects of yoga on mental and physical health: a short summary of reviews. *Evidence-Based Complementary and Alternative Medicine*, 2012.

Cope, S. (2018). *Yoga and the Quest for the True Self*. Bantam.

Feuerstein, G. (2003). *The deeper dimension of yoga*. Boston: Shambhala.

Greenberg, M. T., & Harris, A. R. (2012). Nurturing mindfulness in children and youth: Current state of research. *Child Development Perspectives*, 6(2), 161-166.

Hagen, I., & Nayar, U. S. (2014). Yoga for children and young people's mental health and well-being: research review and reflections on the mental health potentials of yoga. *Frontiers in psychiatry*, 5, 35.

Hobfoll, S. E., Watson, P., Bell, C. C., Bryant, R. A., Brymer, M. J., Friedman, M. J., ... & Maguen, S. (2007). Five essential elements of immediate and mid–term mass trauma intervention: Empirical evidence. *Psychiatry: Interpersonal and Biological Processes*, 70(4), 283-315.

Kaley-Isley, L. C., Peterson, J., Fischer, C., & Peterson, E. (2010). Yoga as a complementary therapy for children and adolescents: a guide for clinicians. *Psychiatry (Edgmont)*, *7*(8), 20.

Khalsa, S. B. S., Hickey-Schultz, L., Cohen, D., Steiner, N., & Cope, S. (2012). Evaluation of the mental health benefits of yoga in a secondary school: A preliminary randomized controlled trial. *The journal of behavioral health services & research*, *39*(1), 80-90.

Lasater, J. H. (2016). *Relax and renew: Restful yoga for stressful times*. Shambhala Publications.

Mason, H., & Gerbarg, P. (2018). Anxiety. In *Yoga for Mental Health*. H. Mason & K. Birch (2019). Scotland: Handspring Publishing Limited.

Porges, S. W. (2009). The polyvagal theory: new insights into adaptive reactions of the autonomic nervous system. *Cleveland Clinic journal of medicine*, *76*(Suppl 2), S86.

Pynoos, R. S., Steinberg, A. M., & Piacentini, J. C. (1999). A developmental psychopathology model of childhood traumatic stress and intersection with anxiety disorders. *Biological psychiatry*, *46*(11), 1542-1554.

Ray, A. (2010). *Yoga and Vipassana: An Integrated Life Style*. Inner Light Publishers.

Robold, L. (2002). Yoga and emotional healing for aggressive youth. *International Journal of Yoga Therapy*, *12*(1), 81-88.

Ross, A., & Thomas, S. (2010). The health benefits of yoga and exercise: a review of comparison studies. *The journal of alternative and complementary medicine*, *16*(1), 3-12.

Tate, A. (2003). Yoga and mental health: Children and adolescents make space in the system for deeper practices. *International Journal of Yoga Therapy*, *13*(1), 83-87.

Tsao, J. C., Meldrum, M., Bursch, B., Jacob, M. C., Kim, S. C., & Zeltzer, L. K. (2005). Treatment expectations for CAM interventions in pediatric chronic pain patients and their parents. *Evidence-Based Complementary and Alternative Medicine*, *2*(4), 521-527.

Van der Kolk, B. (2014). *The body keeps the score: Mind, brain and body in the transformation of trauma*. Penguin UK.

Varma, C., & Raju, P. (2012). Yoga Therapy In Pediatrics.

Weaver, L. L., & Darragh, A. R. (2015). Systematic review of yoga interventions for anxiety reduction among children and adolescents. *American Journal of Occupational Therapy*, *69*(6), 6906180070p1-6906180070p9.

Wei, M. D. J. (2015). 7 Ways Yoga Helps Children and Teens. Psychology Today. (Retrieved 15th, February, 2020).

White, L. S. (2012). Reducing stress in school-age girls through mindful yoga. *Journal of Pediatric Health Care*, *26*(1), 45-56.

Printed in Poland
by Amazon Fulfillment
Poland Sp. z o.o., Wrocław